Thomas Guthrie

Parables Read in the Light of the Present Day

Thomas Guthrie

Parables Read in the Light of the Present Day

ISBN/EAN: 9783744793780

Printed in Europe, USA, Canada, Australia, Japan

Cover: Foto ©ninafisch / pixelio.de

More available books at **www.hansebooks.com**

THE
PARABLES

Read in the Light of the Present Day.

BY

THOMAS GUTHRIE, D. D.,

AUTHOR OF "THE GOSPEL IN EZEKIEL," "THE SAINT'S INHERITANCE," "WAY TO LIFE," "SPEAKING TO THE HEART," ETC.

NEW YORK:
ROBERT CARTER AND BROTHERS,
No. 530 BROADWAY.
1866.

CONTENTS.

INTRODUCTORY...	7
I. THE PARABLE OF THE LEAVEN........................	15
II. " " " " TEN VIRGINS......................	30
III. " " " " PRODIGAL SON.....................	47
IV. " " " " GOOD SAMARITAN....................	73
V. " " " " UNJUST JUDGE......................	97
VI. " " " " PHARISEE AND PUBLICAN............	123
VII. " " " " HID TREASURE......................	149
VIII." " " " PEARL OF THE GREAT PRICE........	171
IX. " " " " LOST PIECE OF MONEY..............	191
X. " " " " SOWER.............................	209
XI. " " " " UNMERCIFUL SERVANT...............	235
XII. " " " " LABORERS IN THE VINEYARD........	261

THE PARABLES

READ IN THE LIGHT OF THE PRESENT DAY.

Introductory.

I ONCE saw Moffat, the South African missionary, address a thousand children—the most formidable congregation, in one sense, before which any speaker could appear. The difficulty, after having aroused their attention, of keeping it awake, was increased on that occasion by two things. His address extended beyond an hour, and the time was evening, when sleep is so apt to fall on young eyes; yet there was not a sleeper in the whole house. The sea of young faces was all turned radiant on the orator; he was the centre for two thousand eager glancing eyes; and for more than the time usually occupied by a sermon he held his audience by the ears. It was a great achievement: and how accomplished? In a very simple way. Suiting the action to the word, and drawing on his own observation and experience, he told them stories, illustrative of the labors and purposes, of the difficulties and dangers of a missionary's life. In giving this form to an address which was not childish, though suited to children, he dexterously availed himself of one of the strongest and earliest developed principles of our nature. How often have I seen a restless boy, whom neither threats nor bribes could quiet, sit spell-bound by a nursery tale! We can all recollect the time when we sat listening to a mother's or nurse's stories for long hours around the winter hearth. So passes the time with the soldier by his watch-fire; with the sailor on the lonely deep; and so, when the day's journey is done, and tents are pitched, and they have had their evening meal, the Bedouin, seated beneath a starry sky, on the sands of the silent desert, will spend half the night.

Now, parables are just stories; they are told for instruction through means of entertainment; and when Moffat, by anecdotes, analogies, and illustrations, sought to win the attention of his hearers, and convey truth into their hearts, as the arrow, by help of its feathers, goes right to the mark, he was only copying his Master. No addresses recorded in history, common or sacred, have so much of the parable character as our Lord's. Not dry bones, nor, though skillfully put together, mere naked skeletons, they are clothed with flesh and instinct with life. Man has a threefold character: he is a being possessed of reason, of affection, and of imagination; he has a head, a heart, and a fancy. And now proving, and now painting, and now persuading, our Lord's discourses, unlike dry and heavy sermons, along with the strongest arguments, the most pointed and powerful appeals, are full of stories, illustrations, and comparisons; and by this circumstance, as well as by the divinity of his matter, and the blended mildness and majesty of his manner, we explain the fact that Jesus was the prince of preachers,—one whom the common people heard gladly, and who, in the judgment even of his enemies, spake as never man spake. The suitableness of this style of preaching a gospel, intended as well for the unlearned as the learned, for converting the unlettered poor, whose souls are as precious in God's sight as those of philosophers or kings, is obvious; and was well expressed by an humble woman. Comprehending best, and most interested and edified by those passages of Scripture which present abstract truth under concrete forms, and of which we have examples in such comparisons of our Lord's as these—the kingdom of heaven is like unto a grain of mustard seed, unto a treasure, unto a merchant, unto a householder, unto a king, she said, "I like best the *likes* of Scripture." These are all parables, a form of speech which our Lord used, indeed so often, and to such an extent, that the evangelists say, "Without a parable spake he not unto them." Occasionally used to conceal for a time the full meaning of the speaker, the chief and common object of a parable is by the story to win attention and maintain it; to give plainness and point, and therefore power, to truth. By awakening and gratifying the imagination, the truth finds its way more readily to the heart, and makes a deeper impression on the memory. The story, like a float, keeps it from sinking; like a nail, fastens it in the mind; like the feathers of an arrow, makes it strike, and, like the barb, makes it stick.

While parables differ from fables, also a very ancient form of speech and instruction, in this, among other things, that fables use the fanciful machinery of beasts and birds and trees, they are allied to proverbs and allegories. They are stories of events that may or may not have happened, but told for the purpose of conveying important truths in a lively and striking manner. They need not be in words, they may be acted; and sometimes men inspired of God, have, instead of telling, acted them with dramatic power. Go, said the Lord to Jeremiah, and get a potter's earthen bottle, and take of the ancients of the people, and of the ancients of the priests; and go forth unto the valley of the son of Hinnom, and proclaim there the words that I shall tell thee. To his summons they assemble, and the preacher appears—nor book, nor speech in hand, but an earthen vessel. He addresses them. Pointing across the valley to Jerusalem, with busy thousands in its streets, its massive towers and noble temple glorious and beautiful beneath a southern sky, he says, speaking as an ambassador of God, I will make this city desolate and an hissing: every one that passeth thereby shall be astonished and hiss: I will cause them to eat the flesh of their sons and the flesh of their daughters, in the siege and straitness wherewith their enemies and they that seek their lives shall straiten them. He pauses—raises his arm—holds up the potter's vessel—dashes it on the ground; and planting his foot on its shivered fragments, he adds, Thus saith the Lord of Hosts, Even so will I break this people, and this city, as one breaketh a potter's vessel. The scene, the aspect of the man, the beautiful but fragile vase, the crash, the shivered fragments, these, all-important aids to the speaker, were calculated to make an impression through the senses and the fancy, much deeper than the mere message could have done.

After the same manner, we find another acting his parable, charged also with a burden of coming sorrows. To the amazement of the people, setting them all a wondering what he could mean, Ezekiel appears one day before them with fire, a pair of scales, a knife, and a barber's razor. These were the heads, and doom was the burden of his sermon. Sweeping off, what an Eastern considers it a shame to lose, his beard, and the hair also from his head, this bald and beardless man divides them into three parts; weighing them in the balance. One third he burns in the fire; one third he smites with the knife; and the remaining third he tosses in the air, scattering it on the winds of heaven. Thus—he himself representing the Jewish nation; his hair the people; the razor the Chaldeans; the cutting off of the hair impending national disgrace; the balances, God's righteous judgment; the part burnt, those destroyed in the city; the part smitten with the knife, those slain when attempting to escape; and the remaining part scattered to the winds, the dispersion of the survivors,—by this acted parable, and in a way most likely to imprint the truth on their memories and impress it on their hearts, he foretells the desolations that were impending over them.

The parable may assume a variety of forms, but the rule of interpretation is the same in all cases. The nearer we can make everything in the parable apply, and stand out as the medium of an important truth, so much the better. But while there may be a meaning in many of the circumstances, the clothing, as you might say, of the story—and it is our business to find that out—any attempt to regard everything as charged with a distinct meaning, to find a spiritual truth in each minute circumstance, would often land us in the regions of fancy; and sometimes in those of error. Take, for example, the parable of the Rich Man and Lazarus. Our Lord represents Abraham and Dives as talking to each other across the gulf which yawns, unbridged, between heaven and hell. But are we to infer from this that the intercourse of this world is maintained in the other, and that sights or sounds of misery disturb the blessed rest of the saints of God? Certainly not. It would be as contrary also to all that we believe, to infer from the rich man expressing a desire for the welfare of the brothers he had left behind him, that virtues grow amid these fires which grew not in the more genial clime of earth. The lost are not certainly improved by their association with devils. If the longer in prison the greater criminal, the longer in perdition the greater sinner! The dead fruit grows more rotten, and the dead body more loathsome in its change to dust; even so they that are filthy shall not only be filthy, but shall be filthier still.

Take another example in the parable of the Ten Virgins. I read that as a solemn warning. It calls us to be up and doing; to hold ourselves ready for the Lord's coming, since we know neither the day nor the hour the Bridegroom may come; to work while it is called to-day, seeing how the night cometh when no man can work—when shops are shut, and there is no oil to buy. But if, allowing nothing for what might be called the drapery of the story, we are to find divine truth set forth not only in the main but in the minor circumstances, in every particular of the parable, see where this leads us! There were five wise and five foolish; five taken in, and five shut out, to whose applications for admission, and earnest, long, loud knocking no answer came but, The door is shut. The first five represent the saved, and the second the lost. But are we to infer, since the number of the wise and the foolish virgins was equal, that the lost are as numerous as the saved? This would be a dreadful, and, I venture to say, a very rash conclusion. Nowhere has God revealed such solemn secrets. Our Lord rebuked the curiosity that asked, Are there few that be saved? —replying, Strive to enter in at the strait gate, for many, I say unto you, will seek to enter in, and shall not be able. To force such an utterance from the parable, to conclude because there was an equal number of wise and foolish virgins, that the lost are as numerous as the saved, has no warrant in the Word of God, and is contrary to the ideas we fondly cherish of Christ's final, glorious, and most triumphant conquest. If, at the close of the war, Satan retains half his kingdom, his head is not crushed, nor, if he carries off half his forces from the battle-field, is he defeated, as I would hope he shall be. We cling to the hope that equal numbers will not stand on the right and on the left hand of the Judge, and that the wail of misery, piercing as it is, shall be drowned and lost in the louder burst of praise. It were a sad account of any government were half its subjects immured in prison; and I would not believe without the strongest evidence that under the reign of a benign and merciful God, and notwithstanding the blood poured out on Calvary, half the inhabitants of a world are lost upon which the Saviour descended on wings of love, while his angel escort sang, Glory to God in the highest, and on earth peace, good will toward men.

In explaining a parable, what we are therefore to seek is its great central truth, the one, two, or three grand lessons which the story was told to teach—setting aside such parts as are no more than color, clothing, drapery thrown around it, to impart life and interest. Keeping this in view, let us now turn to study this woman at her household work, and learn the lesson that she teaches.

I.
The Parable of the Leaven.

"The kingdom of heaven is like unto leaven, which a woman took and hid in three measures of meal, till the whole was leavened."—MATTHEW xiii. 33.

THE Kingdom of Heaven is sometimes used in Scripture as equivalent to the kingdom of God, but it has not here the wide meaning of that expression. There are kingdoms, our own for instance, which embrace so many different and such distant countries, that, as is said and boasted of, the sun never sets on them—before he has set on one province he has risen on another. But how much greater the kingdom of God? The sun never sets on it! The sun never rose and shone but on a corner of it. Its provinces are not countries, nor even continents, but worlds. It stretches not from shore to shore, but from sun to sun, and from star to star. Its extent was never surveyed; its inhabitants never numbered; its beginning never calculated. It had no beginning, and it has no bounds. Its beginning is in eternity, and its bounds are lost in illimitable space. Over this kingdom, which includes heaven and hell, the angels that kept and those that lost their first estate, all things visible and invisible, Jehovah reigns—glorious in counsel, fearful in praises, continually doing wonders. Sole monarch of this empire, he has made all things for himself, yea, "he hath made the wicked for the day of evil."

It is not of this, but of the gospel kingdom, or the kingdom of grace, that the parable speaks; and before showing how it is like leaven, we may turn our attention on some of its peculiar characteristics.

Different and distinct from that kingdom of Jehovah's power and providence, which embraces all created beings from angels down to insects, this has men alone for its subjects. It does not concern itself, unless indirectly, with matter, but only with mind; controlling not the waves of the sea or the winds of heaven, but what are more uncontrollable than either, the passions and wills of men. Again, this kingdom is felt, but not seen; "the kingdom of God cometh not with observation:" it is in the world, but not of it; "My kingdom is not of this world," said Jesus; "if my kingdom were of this world, then would my servants fight:" a spiritual kingdom, its foundations have been laid in the death of its King, and with a far higher object than any for which mortal men are raised to tottering thrones, its purpose is the salvation of lost, but precious and immortal souls.

See how many and important differences there are between it and any earthly kingdom! There never was a man born in it; but many have been born for it. Its subjects are all twice born; for "except a man be born again, he cannot enter into the kingdom of heaven." Never in a sense did an old man enter its gates; for who would enter here must retrace his steps along the path of life; return the way he came, and born again, become a little child. Calling a little child to him, Jesus set him in the midst of them, and said, Verily I say unto you, Except ye be converted, and become as little children, ye shall not enter into the kingdom of heaven. There gold, for which so many here slave, and drudge, and scheme, and sin, is reckoned of no more value than common dust. They buy and sell, indeed; buy the most precious wares, bread of life, immortal beauty, sinless purity, pearls of great price, and crowns of eternal glory; but then it is without money—what is priceless is got without price, got for the asking: "Whatsoever ye ask in my name believing, ye shall receive." And so far from gold being of any advantage here, it is rather an incumbrance than otherwise: "It is easier," said the King, "for a camel to pass through the eye of a needle, than for a rich man to enter the kingdom of heaven." Nor is that which secures man great advantages here, industry, sobriety, honor, honesty, or virtue, any passport into this kingdom; the worst are as welcome as the best: "Whosoever cometh unto me," says the King, "I will in no wise cast out." Beggars whom armed sentinels would challenge, and servants turn from the gates of earthly palaces, are here admitted as freely as the highest nobles. See there, outside the gate, the Pharisee! while the poor, despised, detested publican, who stood afar off, beating his breast in conscious guilt, is invited in, and, going down to his house justified rather than the other, sings with Hannah, "The Lord bringeth low and lifteth up; he raiseth up the poor out of the dust, and lifteth up the beggar from the dunghill, to set them among princes." Yes, this is the kingdom for the poor! In its palace there are more peasants to be met than peers; many subjects and few kings. In your earthly kingdoms the rich and noble carry off the lion's share. It is high-born men and women that fill high places, and stand near our Queen's throne; but this kingdom bestows its noblest honors on the humble, the poor, the obscure, the meek, the lowly; for "to the poor the gospel is preached," and "not many mighty, not many noble are called." More extraordinary than any of these things, all the ordinary rules of other kingdoms are reversed in this. Here, the way to grow rich is to become poor—the path to honor lies through shame—to enjoy rest we must plunge into a sea of troubles—peace is only to be enjoyed in a state of war—who would live must die—and who would gain must part with all that men hold most dear: Verily, verily, says the King, there is no man that leaveth father, or mother, or wife, or children, or houses, or lands, for the kingdom of God's sake, who shall not receive manifold more in this life, and in the world to come life everlasting. Blessed are they who have been brought into this kingdom! Robed in the white linen of Christ's righteousness, they shall be priests, and, crowned with glory, they shall be kings to God.

In regard to the leaven to which our Lord likens the kingdom of heaven, it may surprise some to find that which is usually employed in a bad sense otherwise employed here. I am aware that leaven is often, and indeed usually, in the Sacred Scriptures, an emblem of sin; and a very suitable one it is, seeing, as is known to all who are familiar with its action in household or other arts, that it changes the natural properties of those substances on which it acts, breeds in liquids a poisonous gas, and applied to meal, for instance, swells it up and sours it. But to infer from this that leaven stands here for unsound doctrine and ungodly practice, and that the parable itself is a prophetic description of the corruptions which early crept into the Church of Christ, and had leavened and corrupted the whole mass of Christendom in the dark ages of Popery, were inconsistent with the plain meaning of the parable; and is not required by the rules which should guide us in studying the Word of God. There are other instances in which the sacred writers employ a figure, sometimes in a good sense, sometimes in a bad one. For example, Satan is compared to a lion; and what emblem could be more appropriate, if you take into account its cruel nature, its stealthy approach, its frightful roar, its terrible aspect, its bloody jaws, its ravenous appetite, and the death that follows a blow of its paw? Yet if the destroyer of souls is a lion, so is their Saviour; he is "the Lion of the tribe of Judah." The other most common scriptural emblem of the devil is a serpent. It was in the form of that reptile he stole into Eden; and, with malice gleaming in its fiery eye, poison concealed in its crooked fangs, fascination in its gaze, death in its spring; and this peculiar habit, that while other creatures usually content themselves with a portion of their prey, the serpent, crushing the bones and covering the body with slime, swallows it entire—the animal world furnishes no creature that represents so well the deceiver and destroyer of souls as this hateful, horrid reptile. But who, on the other hand, does not know that a serpent was employed as a type of the Redeemer? Referring to that scene in the desert, where, raised high upon a pole, the brazen serpent gleamed over the dying camp, and whosoever caught sight of it revived and lived, our Lord says, As Moses lifted up the serpent in the wilderness, even so must the Son of man be lifted up, that whosoever believeth in him should not perish, but have eternal life.

Having removed a difficulty which has staggered some and set others on a wrong track, we are now ready to see in what respects the kingdom of heaven is like unto the leaven which this woman takes and hides in meal till the whole is leavened. We may understand our Lord as describing either the influence of the gospel on the world, and its final universal manifestation; or the influence and operation of divine grace on those in whose hearts the Spirit of God has lodged it. The parable may be applied either way; but we prefer the latter.

I.

The woman takes the leaven to lay it not on, but in the meal, where, working from within outwards, it changes the whole substance from the centre to the surface. It is through a corresponding change that the man goes to whom the Spirit of God communicates his grace. It is hidden in the heart. The change

begins there; the outward reformation not preparing the way for regeneration, but springing from it; growing out of it as a tree grows out of its seed, or a stream flows out of its spring. Observe that this view is in perfect harmony with God's requirement, "Give me"—not thy habits, or thy service, or thy obedience, but "thy heart, my son;" in perfect harmony, also, with his promise, "I will take away the stony heart out of your flesh, and I will give you an heart of flesh, and I will put my Spirit within you"—then, as following such a change, "I will cause you to walk in my statutes, and ye shall keep my judgments and do them;" and in perfect harmony also with the remarkable saying of our Lord, "The kingdom of God is within you;" in other words, religion does not lie in the denomination we belong to, in attendance on churches whose stony fingers point to heaven, in having a pew in the house of God, or even an altar in our own, in professions of piety, or even in works of benevolence. It lies in the heart. If it is not there, it is nowhere; these other things being but the dress which may drape a statue, and give to a corpse the guise, or rather the mockery of life. In consequence of its being lodged in their hearts, true Christians, so far from being hypocrites, have more of the reality of religion than of its appearance. They are better than they seem to be; and less resemble those fruits which, under a painted skin, and soft, luscious pulp, conceal a rough, hard stone, than those within whose shell and husky covering there are both milk and meat. With more religion in his heart than you would infer from outward appearances, or than he is able to carry out in his daily life and conversation but after a long struggle with old habits, a converted man may be like Lazarus, when, standing before his tomb, still bound in grave-clothes, he looked as much like a dead man as a living. Even Paul himself said, The good that I would, I do not; but the evil that I would not, that I do. His heart, burning with love to Christ, set on fire not of hell but heaven, was better than his habits; his desires were purer than his deeds; his aims were loftier than his loftiest attainments. And those who, though it is a confession of shortcoming, can say so of themselves, have good reason to hope that the leaven has been hid in the meal. Their hearts have received that grace which works in holy desires toward holy efforts: and which shall never cease to work till, extending its influence over all their nature, the whole is leavened, and they, however imperfect now, become perfect men in Jesus Christ.

II.

Suppose that the woman, taking instead of leaven, a stone—a piece of granite, a common pebble, or even a precious jewel, or any metal such as gold or silver, or any like inert and inactive substance, had placed that in the heart of the meal, the meal had remained the same; changing neither to stone nor metal. But so soon as leaven is imbedded in its substance, a change immediately ensues; a process of fermentation is set a-going, and, extending from within outwards, goes on till by a law of nature the whole lump is leavened. Neither art nor nature could supply a better simile of the grace of God than this. An active element, so soon as it is lodged in the heart, it begins to work; nor ceases to extend its holy influence over the affections and habits, the inward and outward character, till it has moved and changed the whole man, and that consummation is reached which is to be devoutly wished for, and which the Apostle prays for, in the words, May the very God of peace sanctify you wholly.

There are influences which may powerfully affect without permanently changing us. There may be motion, and even violent emotion, without change. In the valley where Ezekiel stood with the mouldering dead around him, there was motion—the bones were shaken. He saw bone approach bone, till, each nicely fitted to the other, they formed perfect skeletons; and, clothed with flesh and covered over with skin, each seemed a warrior taking his rest, and sleeping on under a wizard's spell till his sword had rusted beside him. Still, in all that was essential they were unchanged; as breathless, lifeless, dead, as when the bones lay scattered, withered, and dry on that old field of battle. To borrow an illustration from familiar objects—the sea which reflects like a liquid mirror ship and boat that lie sleeping on its placid bosom, is thrown by the storms of heaven into the most violent commotion. Its calm depths are stirred, and foaming breakers beat its shore; but it is still the salt, salt sea. And when the wind falls, the storm blows past, and the waves sink to rest, it presents the same characters as before—the tempest came and the tempest went, nor has left one trace behind. So it is, alas, too often and too much with the impressions of sermons, and sacraments, and revival seasons.

All changes truly are not from bad to good, or from good to better. They may be from good to bad, or from bad to worse. Moisture dims the polished blade, and turns its bright steel into dull, red rust; fire changes the sparkling diamond into black coal and gray ashes; disease makes loveliness loathsome, and death converts the living form into a mass of foul corruption. But the peculiarity of grace is this, that like leaven it changes whatever it is applied to into its own nature. For as leaven turns meal into leaven, so divine grace imparts a gracious character to the heart; and this is what I call its assimilating element. Yet let there be no mistake. While the grace of God changes all who are brought in conversion under its influence, it does not impart any new power or passion, but works by giving to those we already have a holy bent; by impressing on them a heavenly character. For example, grace did not make David a poet, or Paul an orator, or John a man of warm affections, or Peter a man of strong impulses and ardent zeal. They were born such. The grace of God changes no more the natural features of the mind than it does those of the body—as the negro said, it gave him a *white* heart, but it left him still, to use the language of another, the image of God carved in ebony. Be the meal into which that woman hides the leaven, meal of wheat or meal of barley, it will come from her hands, from the process of leavening, from the fiery oven; cakes of the same grain. For it is not the substance but the character of the meal that is changed. Even so with the effect of grace. It did not give John his warm affections; but it fixed them on his beloved Master—sanctifying his love. It did not inspire Nehemiah with the love of country; but it made him a holy patriot. It did not give Dorcas a woman's heart, her tender sympathy with suffering; but it associated charity with piety, and made her a holy philanthropist. It did not give Paul his genius, his resistless logic, and noble oratory; but it consecrated them to the cause of Christ—touching his lips as with a live coal from the altar, it made him such a master of holy eloquence that he swayed the multitude at his will, humbled the pride of kings, and compelled his very judges to tremble. It did not give David a poet's fire and a poet's lyre; but it strung his harp with chords from heaven, and tuned all its strings to the service of religion and the high praises of God. So grace ever works! It assimilates a man to the character of God. It does not change the metal, but stamps it with the divine image; and so assimilates all who have received Christ to the nature of Christ, that unless we have the same mind, more or less developed, in us that was in him, the Bible declares that we are none of his.

III.

It is said of the meal in which the woman hid the leaven, that, "the whole," not a portion of it, large or small, "was leavened." The apostle brings out the same diffusive character of this element where he says, "A little leaven leaveneth the whole lump." Even so, teaching us not to despise the day of small things, a little grace lodged in the heart spreads till it sanctify the whole man. Some things diffuse themselves rapidly. There are deadly poisons so rapid and indeed sudden in their action that the cup falls from the suicide's hand; he is a dead man before he has time to set it down. To these grace stands out in striking contrast, not only because it is saving, but because it is ordinarily slow in bringing its work to a holy and blessed close; and in that respect grace and sin correspond well to their figures of life and death. Five hundred summers must shine on an oak ere it attain its full maturity; and not less than twenty or thirty years spent in growth and progress must elapse ere an infant arrives at perfect manhood—ere mind has acquired its full power, and bones and muscles their utmost strength. And besides the lapse of so many years, how much care and watching, how much meat and medicine, are needed to preserve our life, and guard it from the accidents and diseases which are ever threatening its destruction! Yet this work of years it needs but an instant of time, a wrong step, a drop of poison, a point of steel, a pellet of lead, to undo. Death is perfected in a moment; the shriek, the prayer may die unuttered on the lips. Look at Adam! Sin, a sudden as well as subtle poison, shoots like lightning through his soul; and he falls in a moment, in the twinkling of an eye, from the state of a pure and happy, into that of a sinful, and wretched, and lost, and ruined being. Unless in such rare and extraordinary cases as that of the dying thief, what a contrast to this the progress of the best in grace!

Years have come and gone, perhaps, since we were converted, and how many Sabbaths have we enjoyed, how many sermons have we heard, how many prayers have we offered, how many communions have we attended, how many providences have we met to help us on in the divine life—goodnesses that should have led us to repentance, and waves of trouble that should have lifted us higher on the Rock of Ages, and yet, alas! how little progress have we made, how far are we from being perfect as our Father in heaven is perfect! Have we not learned, by sad experience, that there is nothing so easy as to commit sin, and nothing so difficult as to keep out of it—even for one hour to keep the heart holy, and the garment unspotted of the world? It seems as natural for man to fall into sin as it is for water to sink to the lowest level, or for a stone to fall to the earth. But to rise! ah, that requires such sustained and continuous efforts as those by which the lark soars to the skies, through constant beating of its wings. The devil can make man a sinner; nor is there a poor, miserable, mean, wretched creature but may tempt us into sin. But it needs the Almighty God to make a man a saint. The vase, statue, beautiful machine which it required the highest skill and long hours of thought and labor to make, may be shattered by the hands of a madman or of a child.

Still, let God's people thank him, and take courage. Though grace, unlike sin, and like leaven, is slow in its progress, it shall change the whole man betimes; and the motto which flashed in gold on the High Priest's forehead shall be engraven on our reason, heart, and fancy; on our thoughts, desires, and affections; on our lips, and hands, and feet; on our wealth, and power, and time; on our body and soul—the whole man shall be "Holiness to the Lord."

These three characters of grace form three excellent test of character, of the genuineness of our religion. It is internal: have we felt its power within us, on our hearts? It is assimilating: is it renewing us into the likeness of Jesus Christ, into the image of God? It is diffusive: is there a work begun in us, and on us, which shall at length "sanctify us wholly"? If not so, we need to begin at the beginning—by the Holy Spirit of God to be born again. But if so, though in many respects defective, and having often to confess with Paul, "The good which I would I do not, and the evil which I would not, that I do," happy are we! Happy are the people that are in such a case, for the Lord will perfect that which concerneth us—the whole shall be leavened.

Be it our business, by earnest prayer and diligence, to hasten on such a blessed consummation; and also to bring the grace that is within us to act as well without as within! No candle is lighted for itself: no man lights a candle to lock the door, and leave it burning in an empty room. We are not lighted for ourselves; nay, nor leavened for ourselves. No man liveth for himself. Let us be as leaven in our families; among our friends and fellows; in the neighborhoods around us. Nor let us rest till there is not one within the sphere of our influence whom we have not, through God's blessing, leavened, or attempted to leaven, by our grace. Freely we have received; freely give! At the fires of our piety let others be warmed; at the light of our grace, let other lights be kindled. Let us act like leaven on the inert, dead mass around us—every living Christian a centre from which living influence shall emanate toward all around him. Were we so, how soon would the dull mass begin to work, ferment, move, and change! Then would it be seen, to the glory of God, and the well-being of society, and the happiness of many a family, and the saving of many souls, that through the influence of those who had little influence, and seemed to have none, as in the case of an humble domestic, or little child, "a little leaven leaveneth the whole lump."

II.

The Parable of the ten Virgins.

Matthew xxv. 1—13.

THIS parable is founded on a marriage scene. Though—as, for example, in wars, or in the Corinthian games—the Scriptures are not to be regarded as approving of all things which they may employ as figures, approbation and honor are bestowed on marriage by the lofty uses to which the sacred writers turn it. With prophets and apostles it shadows forth the holy, intimate, eternal union which is formed between God's beloved Son and his chosen people. Those who feel a Christian interest in the purity and happiness of society, will not regard that as a circumstance of no value. Such discredit as the Popish Church throws on marriage, by representing it as less holy and honorable than celibacy, and such impediments as pride and ambition throw in its way, should be denounced by those who, as Christian ministers, ought to be Christian moralists,—preaching to the times. One of their most evil features is the false standard of income and position which it is considered proper they who intend to marry should in the first place secure. This has led to the bitterest disappointments; to breach of vows; to broken hearts,—besides being the fruitful source of much crime, and furnishing the licentious with an apology for their immoralities. On this altar, human happiness, as well as the best interests of morality, are offered up in cruel sacrifice. A man's life, as Scripture saith, consisteth not in the abundance of the things which he possesseth,— a dinner of herbs where love is, is better than a stalled ox, and hatred therewith.

The institution which forms the basis of this parable is one of the two, belonging to innocence and Eden, which the Fall that shook the world and turned it, as an earthquake does a city, into a scene of ruins, left standing. These are the Sabbath and Marriage—the first forming the foundation on which religion, and the last that on which the social fabric, stands. And in looking back to the first marriage, I cannot but think that it was to make its tie more tender that God chose the singular plan he pursued in providing the man with a mate. No other way would have occurred to our fancy of making woman than that of another clay figure, modelled by God's hands in the female form, and inspired by his breath with life. In making her out of Adam, and from the part of his body lying nearest to the heart, while he lay in the mysterious sleep from which he woke to gaze on a beautiful form reposing by his side, God gave a peculiar emphasis and power to the figure "they twain shall be one flesh,"—one in sympathy, in mind, in affections, and in interests; nothing but death afterwards to divide them.

Though thus a sacred, marriage was originally a

simple, institution. God married the first couple that were husband and wife; but though it had the sanction, it was not till long ages afterwards that marriage was invested with the ceremonies of religion,—and priests were introduced on the scene. In none of the cases recorded in Scripture did the parties repair to a place of worship, or call on a minister of religion to tie the nuptial knot. Though such a custom might be proper, and did to some extent prevail even among the heathen, it derives no authority from the Word of God; and may, as existing among us, perhaps be traced to our early connection with the Church of Rome. Animated by that insatiable ambition which, grasping at all power, has made her the enemy of the liberties of mankind, she seized on marriage, and, exalting this institution into a sacrament, turned it into a tool to serve her own selfish ends. Having persuaded mankind that there could be no holy or valid union without her sanction, she had the thing she sought, the world at her feet,—and there not peasants only, but crowned kings humbly crouched, soliciting a liberty which God had already granted.

Long years, however, before this institution was invested with religious forms, it had been the custom to celebrate it with festivities,—a custom observed by none more than the Jews. For these joyous and festive habits they had the highest sanction. Our Lord accepted an invitation to a marriage scene, and honored it by the performance of his first miracle; and, though we are to set our hearts on that world where they neither marry nor give in marriage, we should learn from the story of Cana to rejoice with them that do rejoice, as well as to weep with them that weep. It is not religion to turn away from scenes of harmless mirth; such as that on which Jesus put the seal of his approbation, and shed the sunshine of his presence.

It is the last act in the drama of such ceremonies as were observed in Cana of Galilee that this parable presents. The marriage has been celebrated. Accompanied by his bride, the bridegroom is about to return to his own house, their future home. The time, as is still the case in many eastern countries, is night; and the scene has all the picturesque effect of a torchlight procession. While one band of maidens accompany her from her father's house, another wait near the bridegroom's to welcome them home. The hours wear on; eyes peer through the darkness to discover the gleams, and ears listen to catch the sound of the advancing party. By and by, lights sparkle in the distance; by and by, at first faintly heard, shouts and songs break the silence of the night; and now the cry rises, Behold, the bridegroom cometh; go ye out to meet him. All are roused—sleepers wakened, lamps trimmed, torches made to blaze with strong and lively flame; and forth from their places go, trooping, singing, rejoicing, the train of waiting maidens. Mingling with the advancing crowd, above whose heads sit the bridegroom and his bride, in gorgeous attire, their jewels flashing back the gleams of lamp and torch, they pass into the house. And now the door is shut. Those ready enter with the bridegroom; such as are unready are kept out, and to their knocking get no other answer but that of the parable, "I know you not." In considering this parable let us look at

THE BRIDEGROOM.

He represents our Lord Jesus Christ, the divine head and loving husband of that Church which is his bride, "the Lamb's wife,"—the union which faith forms between him and his people being represented as a marriage. It is one of love; for though a wealthy marriage to the bride, it is on her part as well as on his, one of endearment—We love him because he first loved us— Thy people shall be willing in the day of thy power. It is one which grim death shall never dissolve, and leave Christ's Church a mourning widow. It is one which holy prophets sung, and long ages prepared for. It is one which the Son, though stooping to the lowliest object, entered into with his Father's full consent. It is one in which heaven took a part, and angels were wedding-guests,—their harps lending the music and their wings the light. It is one over which all the hosts of heaven rejoiced in the fullness of generous love—I heard, says John, as it were the voice of a great multitude, and as the voice of many waters, and as the voice of many thunderings, saying Alleluiah: for the Lord God omnipotent reigneth. Let us be glad and rejoice, and give honor to him; for the marriage of the Lamb is come, and his wife hath made herself ready. May we know the truth of the words that follow: Blessed are they which are called unto the marriage supper of the Lamb!

The story of redeeming love, of this marriage, surpasses anything related in the pages of the wildest romances. These tell of a prince, who, enamoured of an humble maid, assumed a disguise; and doffing his crown and royal state for the dress of common life, left his palace, travelled far, faced danger, and fared hard, to win the heart of a peasant's daughter, and raise her from obscurity to the position of a queen. Facts, as has been said, are more wonderful than fables. The journey which our divine lover took, was from heaven to earth; to win his bride, he exchanged the bosom of the eternal Father to lie, a feeble infant, on a woman's breast. Son of God, he left the throne of the universe, and assumed the guise of humanity, to be cradled in a manger and murdered on a cross.

Besides, in his people he found a bride, deep in debt, and paid it all; under sentence of death, and died in her room; a lost creature, clad in rags, and he took off his own royal robes to cover her. To wash her, he shed his blood; to win her, he shed his tears; finding her poor and miserable and naked, he endowed her with all his goods; heir of all things, everything that he possessed as his Father's Son, she was to enjoy and share with himself, for are not his people "heirs of God and joint heirs with Christ, if so be that we suffer with him, that we may be also glorified together."

Nor was his a love of yesterday—leaving its object to fear that, mushroom-like, its decay might be as rapid as its growth. Older than the hoary hills, it dated from a period when there were no depths, before the mountains were brought forth;

> "He loved us from the first of time,
> He loves us to the last."

Neither is his love, like man's, capable of coldness or of change; of diminution or decay. Whom he loveth, he loveth to the end. It is stronger than death. Many waters cannot quench it; and no time can cool it. With the fondness of a first love, it has the stability of an old one; what trials does it endure; what ingratitude; what coldness; what contempt! See how he stands at the door knocking, till his head is wet with dew, and his locks with the drops of night! nor counts that anything if he can but win you at the last! And never desisting from pressing his suit on any sinner, lover of our souls, he lingers by the door till another arrive—not with a suit but with a summons—Death himself, come to bear it with a hand that brooks no delay, and takes no refusal.

And why should any refuse the suit of him who stands at their door—a lover, suitor, follower, crying, Behold, I stand at the door and knock—open to me? Setting their affections on unworthy objects, some have repelled addresses which offered them great wealth and high honors; better still, happiness as much as earth can afford. But none ever rejected such an offer as Jesus makes you in the offer of his heart and hand. They never had an opportunity. This the lover of whom it is said, He is the chiefest among ten thousand, he is altogether lovely, his person is the most beautiful, his heart is the kindest, and his bride shall be the happiest and richest the world ever saw—her home a heavenly palace, and her rank higher than any queen's.

Happy are they who have yielded to his suit; and, joining hands with him, have become his in the bonds of the marriage covenant! With the Lord for his shepherd, David felt certain that he could never want, and went down singing into the valley of the shadow of death; but much more may we who, closing with Christ's offer, have given him our hands and received him into our hearts; for how much better does a bridegroom love his blooming bride than shepherd ever loved his sheep? "As the bridegroom rejoiceth over his bride, so shall thy God rejoice over thee."

THE VIRGINS.

Fair women in the prime and flower of life have formed a part, and not the least ornamental part, of nuptial scenes in all ages of the world; and we have still the representatives of the virgins of this parable in the bridesmaids of modern marriages. Ten is their number here. Why ten, and not five, or twenty? The key to this is similar to that which explains the frequent recurrence of seven in the Scriptures—seven golden candlesticks, seven stars in Christ's hand, seven vials, seven plagues, seven thunders; for as the number seven among the Jews denoted perfection, ten was the number that made a thing complete. A company was considered complete when there were ten present—we have Elkanah saying to his wife to comfort her when grieving because she was childless, Am I not better to thee than ten sons? And so also we have the angels of God reckoned as ten times ten thousand. Here, then, blooming like a bed of flowers, are a band of virgins;

beauty in their looks; grace displayed in every movement; joy sparkling in their bright black eyes, and jewels, as they move their lamps to and fro, sparkling in their rich, oriental attire. Now they are watching through the evening hours; now, as the night wears on, slumber falls on their eyelids, and stretching themselves out, one after another, they drop off into sleep; now, roused by the cry of the Bridegroom's coming, all start to their feet to arrange their attire and trim their lamps; now, some revive the dying flames of oil, and others, looking with dismay on empty vessels, with urgency and tears beseech their companions to give them oil. Whom do these represent? Christ is the bridegroom; and the bridesmaids, these virgins, the foolish as well as the wise, who are they?

They stand here the representatives of the visible Church—of every church, and congregation of professing Christians—a picture this which should fill many of us with alarm, and set all to the task of examining the foundation of their hopes, in the view of death and judgment. The five wise virgins are those who are saved at last; the five foolish are those who are lost—and lost, though many of them, at one time, entertained no doubt whatever that they should be saved. They never so much as fancied that they would be shut out. Such a thought never damped their joy, nor disturbed their dreams, as they slept on with dying lamps beside them. Most alarming picture and solemn warning! These poor virgins do not, let it be observed, represent the openly godless; the licentious; the profane; such as are manifestly the enemies, and not the friends of Christ. On the contrary, they could not be, in any plain sense, and were not regarded as, the enemies of the Bridegroom. They had not treated his invitation with contempt; nay, nor even with plain neglect. To some extent they had prepared for his coming; and, till the hour of trial came, they seemed as well prepared to meet the Bridegroom as any of their wise companions. I know nothing in the Bible which more than this parable, and little which so much, should so strongly and so solemnly enforce on us the advice, "Give all diligence to make your calling and election sure."

Unhappy virgins, to whom the Bridegroom brings such unlooked-for woe, who gaze with eyes of horror on your empty lamps, who, with such imploring looks and unavailing tears, entreat aid from your happy companions, who rush out into the darkness only to find the shops all closed, no oil to be bought at so late an hour, who hurry back, alas! to find the door shut—you do not represent hypocrites; or mere formal professors—such as never felt anything of the powers of the world to come; as were never alarmed; never moved by the truth; never thrown into any anxiety about their souls' salvation! Unhappy virgins, at one time all looked so promising—you watched for a while; you had lamps; you had more, you had oil in your lamps; and, though they did not endure, but, unfed, went out, they burned for a time!

Notwithstanding all this, they are lost—teaching us that it is not enough to make a fair appearance; to have been the subjects once of religious impressions;

to have heard the Word of God gladly; to have felt some anxiety about our souls, and to have made some movements in the direction of salvation. We see in them how they who are near to the kingdom may yet never reach it—wrecked at the harbor-mouth, within hail of friends and sight of home. If· such things are done in the green tree, what shall be done in the dry?

Let this case induce every man to prove his own work by such questions as these. Have I been converted? Do I know my heart to be changed? Have I something else to rest on as evidence of being in Christ than merely serious impressions, some occasional good thoughts, and fitful seasons of religious feelings—being well-inclined, to use a common expression? Have I oil not only in the lamp but in the vessel?—in other words, have I the grace of God in my heart?—the love that burns, the faith that endureth to the end? Not he whose light is blown out by every gust of temptation; nor he whose light, a mere lamp of profession, fails amid the trials of death, and, going out, leaves him to darkness and despair; but "he," says our Lord, "that shall endure unto the end, the same shall be saved."

THE SLEEP OF THE VIRGINS.

The scene is one of repose—no sounds but measured breathing; and by the lamps dimly burning, ten forms are seen stretched out in various attitudes, but all locked in the arms of sleep. How unlike sentinels; watchers; persons waiting a Bridegroom's arrival, and ready at any moment for the call to go forth to meet him—they sleep like infants who have nothing to do or care for; or like sons of toil at the close of day, when their day's work is done.

Were even the wise virgins right in yielding to sleep in such circumstances? They are not distinctly blamed; and so far as their own safety was concerned, they suffered no loss by it. With oil not in their lamps only, but in their vessels, being constantly prepared for the Bridegroom's coming, they might go to sleep —they had at least some excuse for sleeping. In one sense, their work was done; and so, in one sense, is ours, if, having received Christ and the grace of God into our hearts, we have made our calling and election sure.

Firstly, The sleep of the wise virgins may indicate that peace which they are invited and entitled to enjoy who have sound, scriptural, indubitable evidence in their hearts and lives, that justified by faith they are at peace with God—and so, as Paul says, may "be careful for nothing." If that is all which is meant by their sleep, let those, whom they represent, sleep on, and take their rest. The peace of God, which passeth all understanding, keep your hearts and minds through Jesus Christ! Never trouble yourselves about death —to you it is gain, and cannot come too suddenly, or too soon. He who lives in Christ is habitually prepared to die; and what more grace is needed for that hour, will come with it. "My God shall supply all your need."

But what is wisdom in some, is folly in others. He may sleep, rocked in the cradle of the billows, whose vessel rides at anchor; not he who is drifting broadside on to the roaring reef. He may sleep who pillows his head on a royal pardon; not he who, pallid and exhausted by the trial; a down-stricken and haggard wretch, enters a cell which he leaves not but for the scaffold, unless he obtain mercy. These foolish virgins ought never to have slept till, applying to the proper quarter, and, if necessary, selling their very jewels for oil, they stood prepared for the Bridegroom's coming. Nor should any rest, seeking their souls' salvation, having it for their first thought in the morning, and their last at night, till they have found it; and obtained a good hope that their sins have been washed away in the blood of the Lamb and Son of God—that God himself is now their Father, and heaven shall be hereafter their blessed home.

Secondly, By the sleeping as well of the wise as of the foolish, our Lord perhaps teaches, what the best will be readiest to admit, that even God's people are not so watchful as they should be; and would be, were they constantly to live under the feeling that they know neither the day nor hour when the Son of Man cometh. Should he come this moment, who, in a sense, are ready to meet him? Are your faith and love, your humility and holiness in as lively exercise; are your thoughts, all your wishes and imaginations, is the tone of your conversation, and the daily tenor of your life, such as you would wish them to be at the Bridegroom's coming? None will say so. Therefore, let us not sleep; nor, with so much to do, act as if we had nothing to do. O, that we could enter on each day's duties, and close each day's work, as if we had possibly seen our last sunrise, or last sunset. That were not a frame of mind inconsistent with earthly enjoyments. No! How bright the sky, how sweet the song of birds, how beautiful the wayside flowers, how full of pleasure everything to that sun-browned man, who expects, in a few more hours, and after long years of exile, to find himself at home.

Besides, these virgins who lie there asleep, ignorant of their wants and insensible to their danger, what reasons do they form for the wise employing the precious hours otherwise than in slumber! It might have proved another night to them had the wise been wakeful. Had they shaken up the sleepers, pointed them to their empty vessels, pleaded with them, and entreated them, while there was time, to go and buy, the lost might have been saved—the door that shut them out might have shut them in. And what true Christian may not have his hands full of such Christ-like work? Among our acquaintances, the members, perhaps, of our families, are there not some who, careless of their souls, and with less appearance of religion than these foolish virgins, are not prepared for a dying hour? They would, I fear, be lost, were the Bridegroom to come now. May the idea of that, of seeing them shut out, hearing their plaintive cries, seeing them stand at the bar of judgment pictures of despair, wringing their hands in hell, saying to themselves, O, if my father, my mother, my brother, my sister, my friend, my minister had only warned me, and pleaded with me, I might never have been here,—haunt us, and lie so heavy on our consciences that we shall find no rest till we have implored them to seek a Saviour,—to flee from the wrath to come. Thus, going to the work in dependence on the Spirit of God, and with the tenderness, gentleness, modesty, and humility of the true Christian love, have many who had neither genius nor intellect been wise to win souls to Christ.

THE SUDDENNESS OF THE BRIDEGROOM'S COMING.

Every stroke which our pulse beats, strikes the knell of a passing soul. There are sixty human lives go out every minute. But while that is the average number, death each day, like the tide, has its flow and ebb. As harmonizing with its gloomy scenes, night is the most common period for dying. She throws her sable veil over the appalling features of life's last struggle. It is most frequently at what is called "the turn of the night," that, in those rooms whose lighted windows contrast with darkened streets, and within whose walls spectators watch through their tears the last throes of expiring nature, the cry arises, Behold, the Bridegroom cometh! At that hour, the cry rose in Egypt when a startled nation woke—and there was not a house in which there was not one dead. So also often on the deep—at midnight, a shock, a crash; and springing from their beds, alarmed passengers rush on deck to see a strange ship vanishing like a phantom in the gloom, and their own, by a gaping wound that admits the sea, sinking into a sudden grave—there is a fearful cry, Behold, the Bridegroom cometh: they wake to hear it, and, sinking, hear no more. How loud and

sudden that cry rose at midnight in the mighty tenement that a year ago shook this city by its fall, and buried in its ruins half a hundred corpses. They slept, nor woke, but to find themselves, to their astonishment, out of this world, and in another—standing before their Judge. How great their surprise; happy if not how great their dismay!

Nor does death surprise its victims only in such accidents. Foreseen by others, how unexpectedly does he often come to the person most concerned! O, the lying that is practised beside many death-beds!—all engaged in a conspiracy to deceive the victim. Verily the tender mercies of the wicked are cruel. Everything serious forbidden; every hint of death forbidden; everything that could excite alarm forbidden,—a dying-chamber is turned into a stage for players, who wipe away their tears before they enter, and wear a lying mask of ease and smiles and hopes, when hope herself is dead. Everybody sees the approach of death, yet not one is found kind and honest enough to speak of it. And they talk of spring who know that its flowers shall bloom on the victim's grave; they talk of journeys who know that these poor feet are journeying onwards to the tomb; they talk of dresses who know that that emaciated form shall wear no robe but the shroud of death,—the whole scene is like that old pageant of heathen worship, where they crowned the lambs with garlands, and led them to the slaughter with dances and music.

In various ways it belongs, if I may say so, to the chapter of accidents, whether our death may not be as sudden and unexpected as the coming of the Bridegroom here; or as the second advent in which our Lord shall appear with the surprise of a thief in the night. What may happen any day, it is certainly wise to be prepared for every day. So men make their wills; but so, alas, they don't mind their souls! This ye should have done, but not have left the other undone. There is no lawyer, but, if you have any property to dispose of, and would not have your death the signal for quarrels and lawsuits and heart-burnings, will advise you to make a settlement, nor delay one day to do so. O, how much more need to make your peace with God, and prepare your eternal rather than your temporal affairs for death,—to make it all up with him who is willing to forgive all, and is now tarrying on the road to give you time to get oil, and go forth with joy to the cry, Behold, the Bridegroom cometh! Seek Christ this day—this hour—this moment. On its decision may hang your irrevocable, fixed, eternal destiny. There is hope for you now; to-morrow there may be none.

III.

The Parable of the Prodigal Son.

Luke xv. 11—32.

YEARS ago, a traveler found himself in a fishing town, where he intended to pass the night. The sun had gone down on a sea of glass; but, as the night fell, the wind began to moan, and ere long a glaring flash and rattling peal announced the storm that broke out over sea and land with tremendous fury. By and bye, the voices of men and women were heard in the streets—mingling with the roar of the tempest. There was none to answer his call; and surprised to find himself the only tenant of the inn, he sallied forth to join the crowd, which, seized with a terrible alarm, and consisting chiefly of old men, women, mothers, and little children, was hurrying to the shore. Their fathers, children, husbands, brothers, had gone off to the fishing; and must now be running for the haven through that black night and roaring sea. There, drenched with rain and the salt spray, clinging to wall, rock, and each other, a crowd was gathered, over which, as they stood, some looking seaward, and some in silent prayer to heaven, a blazing fire, kindled at the pier-end, threw fitful and ruddy gleams. Another light, gleaming like a star over the waves, with which it rose and sank, shone from a life-boat that gallant hands had rowed out to the tail of a reef, between which and the pier the boats must run to make the harbor's mouth. Could they live in such a sea? If they did, could they, guided by these lights, dash through between the shore on this side and the reef on that? Some hoping, some despairing, but all straining their eyes to pierce the gloom, two hours of terrible suspense drag on; at length a faint cheer is raised, as, dimly seen, the headmost boat is descried running for the harbor. They hold their breath—prayers are on their lips, and lives are in that helmsman's hand. Lying on the rudder, he steers her aright. She clears the point of danger; and, as the forms of the boat's crew flash by in the gleam of the pine-wood fire, there is a scream—a voice cries, "It is he! it is he! he's safe!"—and a woman, who had caught sight of her husband in the boat, fell fainting, for very joy, into an old man's arms.

No wonder the stranger, careless of the tempest, mingled with that eager crowd; for, where such a scene was transacting, and men's lives were in the greatest jeopardy, and human bosoms were agitated by as great a tumult as roared above in the stormy skies, and in the waves of that foaming sea, who could sit to enjoy the comforts of a bright fireside and curtained room? Where men's lives, their souls, or great interests are in danger, nothing is so exciting as to watch the uncertain issue; or more gratifying than to see life saved—the dead alive, the lost found. To such stirring sights men and women crowd; to such tales old age, as well as childhood, turns with ear intent.

To this, in part, the parable of the Prodigal, with its strong lights and shadows, with the wickedness of the son, and the father's kindness, forgiveness, and touching joy over one who had been lost and was found, owes the universal interest with which it is read; and the garland with which men have agreed to crown it as, both for the beauty of its story, and the importance of its truths, the finest of all the parables.

THE OCCASION OF THE PARABLE.

The sceptre shall not depart from Judah, nor a lawgiver from between his feet, until Shiloh come—so said the dying Jacob. In accordance with that old prophecy, the Jewish State, at Christ's advent, merged into the Roman Empire; and was, in consequence, taxed to maintain a foreign, and what was particularly offensive to the Jews, a heathen government. The parties employed in raising this public revenue, and who were therefore called publicans, were obnoxious to every pious and patriotic Jew. Some were heathens; and such as were not, being regarded as traitors, were held in double abhorrence—the very beggars refused their charity. With few exceptions, no man of character would accept the office. Excluded from the ranks of respectable society, the publicans acquired the habits of the dregs amongst which they sank; and associated in fact, as well as in common speech, with fallen women, they became notorious for their vices.

Orpheus is said to have drawn savage beasts around him by the charms of music; but our Lord so charmed the world by his preaching, that he drew to him, in publicans and sinners, multitudes more brutal than the beasts. Finding in him a Jew who did not hate but love them, despise but pity them, trample them beneath his feet but stooped to raise them, as if each were a diamond sparkling in the mud, they gathered in crowds to hear him, and listen to one who offered mercy, and held out the flag of hope even to publicans and sinners. The Pharisee, as he swept in full sail to the Temple to thank God that he was not as these, dreading their touch, said, Stand aside; I am holier than thou! Not so Jesus Christ—abhorrent to his holy nature as was their impiety and impurity! Passing like a sunbeam through the foulest atmosphere without pollution, touching pitch and not defiled, breathing infected air but proof against contagion, he rather sought than shunned the company of publicans and sinners. Where should he be found, who came to save, but in the thick of the lost? The selfish, bigoted, narrow-minded Jew, who would have none saved but himself, took offence at this: This man, they said, "receiveth sinners and eateth with them;" and, by way of reproach, they called him "a friend of publicans and sinners."

We accept the picture. Each time heaven's gate is thrown open, he receiveth a sinner; and what keeps our hopes alive, and in the solemn prospect of death or judgment inspires us with any degree of fortitude, but that we shall fall into the hands of him who is "the friend of sinners?" These Pharisees did not understand Jesus Christ any more than vice understands virtue, or blindness colors. Ignorant of his mission, they could not comprehend how one who was holy should rather seek than avoid the lost and reprobate. And it was to reveal the riches of gospel grace, God's purpose of mercy, and the delight he has in converting and saving the greatest sinners, that, with the other parables of this chapter, Jesus told the story of the prodigal.

Regarding the son here as a type of man, and the father as a type of God, as he is seen in his Son and set forth in the gospel, let us now study these, the two prominent figures in this beautiful parable—beginning with the Prodigal.

HIS CONDUCT.

In the case of entailed estates, and in every case where a man in our country dies without leaving a will, the heritable property, according to what is called feudal law, belongs to the eldest son. By the udal law, as in Norway, the whole estate is divided equally among the members of the family. The Jewish law, as appears by the book of Deuteronomy, held a middle course between these two. If a man had two sons, as was the case here, his goods were divided into three parts—two of them falling to the eldest; but to his effects as thus divided, the children did not succeed till the father died.

Tired waiting in his father's death for an event which some sons have hastened, and impatient to possess the means of indulging vices into which we have seen others leave a father's grave to plunge, carelessly scattering what he had too carefully gathered, this youth requests, or rather demands, such share of the property as would by law fall to him at the father's death. Fancy this father's case yours; your feelings at such unnatural and insolent conduct! What a shock to him to find that in his son's heart all home affections were dead, and that he himself was no longer regarded with love, or his gray hairs with respect! The father's presence, and the virtuous habits of a pious home, have become an irksome restraint. This youth would be his own master—rid of his father's strict, pious, and old-fashioned ways of keeping God's law and day; and so, type of man whose heart sin has estranged from God, so soon as his request is granted, he turns his back on home, and takes his departure to a far country.

The father did not compel his son to remain; nor does God us, or indeed any of his creatures. In Eden he left our first parents to the freedom of their own will. There man sought to be independent of God; and here, in the condition of the prodigal, we have a picture of the misery into which sin, having estranged us from our heavenly Father, has plunged its wretched votaries. Devoured by harlots, the portion was soon spent. Want followed on the heels of waste. Driven by hard necessity to become a swineherd, he accepted the meanest, and to a Jew the most degrading employment. A stranger in a strange land; cast away as an orange when men have sucked it; turned off, as I have seen a poor, ragged wretch, from the drinking-shop where he had wasted his means; neglected by old associates; laughed at as a fool by many, and pitied by none, he is reduced to the direst extremity. None offering him better fare, he tries to satisfy his hunger with swine-husks. Type of the sinner who departs from God, and a beacon to such as feel irksome under the restraints of a pious home, he seeks happiness to find only misery—ambitious of an unhallowed liberty, he sinks into the condition of the basest slave.

HIS CHANGE OF MIND.

The words, "He came to himself," here employed to describe the change on the prodigal, imply that he had been beside himself—acting the part of a madman or a fool.

He had the best of fathers; and was not he a fool to leave him?—as if among these vile women and boon companions there were any to love him as his father had done! In a home where he had rings and robes, servants to attend and fatted calves to feed him, music and dancing, when he was sad, to cheer him, was not he a fool to leave it?—as if in a far country, and in the haunts of vice, he would find any place like home. When from the last height that commanded a view of home, he looked back, casting a lingering look behind, was not he a fool, as he suppressed the rising of old affections, and the fancy that he heard the voice of his dead mother calling him back, to dash the tear from his eye, and rush, like a war-horse plunging into the battle, headlong on a course of dissipation—blind to the wretchedness which ever terminates a career of vice?

"The path of transgressors is hard"—to this, God, using his sufferings for the purpose, was pleased to open his eyes. Saved beside the swine-troughs, his sorest misery, as in other cases, proved his greatest mercy. Left to chew the cud of bitter reflection, sitting where all his bones through his rags did look and stare on him, the past, with its sin and folly, rose up before his eyes. O, what a fool he had been! He was convinced of that; and of this also, that to remain there was to die—that it were better to return, and cast himself on his father's pity; better to be his servant than the drudge and slave he was; better to go and unburden his conscience, and acknowledge his wickedness, though he should die at his father's feet. Feeling thus, humbled and penitent, prepared to accept thankfully the smallest favor, and if he is forgiven to be content even with a servant's place, he is now like a maniac restored to reason; as is said, "He came to himself." Happy all of whom the same can be said!

Sin is represented here as a madness; and who acts so contrary to sound reason, his own interests, and the reality of things, as a sinner? Transport yourself to such scenes as Hogarth painted. Here is a man in a damp, dark cell, seated on a heap of straw, and chained like a wild beast to the wall. Does he weep? Is he haunted by recollections of a happy home? Does he, as you look through the bars, entreat you to take pity on him, to loose his fetters, and let him go free? No. He smiles, sings, laughs—the straw is a throne; this bare cell, a palace; these rough keepers, obsequious courtiers; and he himself, a monarch, the happiest of mortals; an object of envy to crowned kings. Strange and sad delusion! Yet, is that man not more beside himself who, with a soul formed for the purest enjoyments, delights in the lowest pleasures; who, content with this poor world, rejects the heaven in his offer; who, surest sign of insanity, hates in a heavenly Father and his Saviour, those who love him; who, in love with sin, hugs his chains; lying under the wrath of God, is merry; sings, and dances on the thin crust that, ever and anon breaking beneath the feet of others, is all that separates him from an abyss of fire? The spectacle recalls the words of Solomon: "I said of laughter, it is madness; of mirth, what doth it?" Happy, such as, through the Spirit of God, working by whatever means, have come to themselves, like the prodigal; and are seated, like the maniac who dwelt among the tombs, at the feet of Jesus, clothed and in their right mind!

HIS DISTRESS.

I perish, he said, with hunger. Dreadful fate!—a death attended with pangs that have turned the softest hearts to stone, and even women into savage beasts. Maddened by hunger, the mother has forgot her sucking child, that she should not have compassion on the fruit of her womb. But how much worse the condition of him of whom the wretched prodigal is a type! The pleasures of sin can never satisfy the cravings of an immortal soul—far less save it. The pangs of the body, besides, come to an end; in the grave, that poor, emaciated form hungers no more, and thirsts no more, and shivers no more—but the wrath of God abideth forever. "Their worm dieth not, and their fire is not quenched." Awful words!—made more awful by the circumstance that they came from the lips of a tender and compassionate Redeemer; and were by him repeated thrice—hammered, if I may say so, into the mind, as a nail is driven to the head by successive blows. Besides, if a man is dying of hunger, he feels it, or of thirst, he feels it; but the misery of a sinner is not to know his misery. Here the type of the prodigal fails. I offer a man the bread of life, and he tells me he is not hungry; living water, and he puts aside the cup, saying, I am not thirsty; I find him stricken down with a mortal disease, but, on bringing a physician to his bed-side, he bids us go, and not disturb him, but leave him to sleep, for he feels no pain. Insensibility to pain is his worst symptom, fatal proof that mortification has begun, and that, unless it can be arrested, all is over—you may go, make his coffin, and dig him a grave. But let sensibility return, so that on pressure being applied to the seat of disease, he shrinks and shrieks out with pain; alarmed and ignorant, his attendants may imagine that now his last hour is come, but the man of skill knows better. There is life in that cry—it proves that the tide has turned, that he shall live. Sign as blessed, when brought to a sense of his sins, a man feels himself perishing; cries with Peter, sinking among the waves of Galilee, I perish; with the prodigal, sitting by the swine-troughs, I perish; with the jailer, at midnight in the prison, What shall I do to be saved? Have we ever felt thus? A most important question! For unless we have felt ourselves lost, we have not yet been saved, and have yet to be converted. Happy such as are so! And as to those who are still far from God, let them arise, with the prodigal, and go to their Father. He waits for them. I promise them the kindest welcome—in his heart there is love, and in his house "bread enough, and to spare."

HIS BELIEF.

I perish! cried the poor prodigal. Why should I? Behind yonder blue hills, away in the dim distance, lies my father's house—a house of many mansions and such full supplies that the servants, even the hired servants, have bread enough, and to spare.

Is there in Jesus Christ a provision as ample for our wants—for the wants of every humble, returning, believing penitent? I might reply by asking, who ever sat at God's table without finding not only bread enough, but to spare? Go back to the days when Israel was in the wilderness. The camp is astir with early dawn. Men, women, and little children troop forth, in the gray morning, to gather the manna that, type of the blessings of salvation, has dropped from bountiful skies on the desert sands. And, when these millions are supplied, there is bread to spare, more meat than mouths—the sun, shooting up, shines on the gleanings of the harvest, as on the hoar-frost of a grassy lawn. Or look at another feast, where five thousand guests are met on a mountain-side, with its green sward for their carpet, the azure sky for a canopy, the twelve apostles for attendants, and Jesus Christ for their host, and master of the feast! In three loaves and some small fishes, the provision does not look Godlike—the counterpart of the desert's daily banquet. The disciples are ashamed; the guests astonished. But our Lord stands up unabashed, and calm in conscious power, up to the blue heavens he turns his eyes; and, his voice sounding clear over silent thousands, he asks a blessing on the scanty meal. Again there is bread enough, and to spare—and these few loaves and fishes, after feeding five thousand hungry guests, fill twelve baskets with their fragments.

In their divine fullness, the desert manna, the mountain fare, were substantial symbols of the mercy, pardon, peace, holiness, and happiness stored up in Christ. Yes. We also can say, there is enough and to spare—for my needs, grace enough; for my sorrows, comfort enough; for my nakedness, raiment enough, and to spare; in that fountain filled from Immanuel's veins, blood enough to wash away my sins, and the sins of the whole world, would the world come to Jesus — but listen to the voice of babes, as they sweetly sing—

> "Come to Jesus, come to Jesus;
> He will save you, he will save you
> Just now.
>
> "O believe him, O believe him,
> O believe him, O believe him,
> Just now."

HIS RESOLUTION.

I will arise, said the prodigal, and go to my father, and say unto him, Father, I have sinned against heaven and before thee! He might well say so. I can detect in him no redeeming trait but one. When he had brought himself to poverty, he had—the fruit of early training—too much honor to beg, and too much honesty to steal, and independence enough to be willing to earn his own bread by stooping to the humblest employment. Better a hard bed, humble fare, and rags that are our own, than to live preying on others, or shining with borrowed splendor!

View it, however, in what light you may, his conduct had been atrociously bad. He preferred the company of harlots to his father's society, and songs of lewd revelry to the melody of his father's worship; a thorn in the old man's side, he had well nigh broken his loving heart, and brought down his gray hairs with sorrow to the grave. There are more dreadful sights than that which filled Jacob with horror when, spreading out the blood-stained garment, Joseph's brothers said, Is this thy son's coat, or no? A dissipated son is a greater trial than a dead one; and more bitter the tears shed over the wreck of such an one's character than those which bedew the coffin where his dead brother lies. Such were the tears this father shed, as with many a bitter thought and agonizing prayer he followed the wanderer, whose name he never mentioned but in secret to his God.

Remove the prodigal, and setting Conscience on the

bench, let us take his place! As sinners against our heavenly Father, who is not as bad as he? Be not offended, or mistake my meaning! We may never have proved thorns in a father's flesh, cost his eye one tear, or a mother's heart a groan—giving them occasion to wish that, lifted from a cradle to a coffin, we had been buried in an early grave. Still, no prodigal ever sinned against an earthly, as we have done against our heavenly Father.

I can measure parental love—how broad, and long, and strong, and deep it is. It is a sea—a deep sea, which mothers and fathers only can fathom. But the love displayed on yonder hill and bloody cross where God's own Son is perishing for us, nor man nor angel has a line to measure. The circumference of the earth, the altitude of the sun, the distance of the planets—these have been determined; but the height, depth, breadth, and length of the love of God passeth knowledge. Such is the Father against whom all of us have sinned, a thousand and a thousand times! Walk the shore when ocean sleeps in the summer calm, or, lashed into fury by the winter tempest, is thundering on her sands; and when you have numbered the drops of her waves, the sands on her sounding beach, you have numbered God's mercies and your own sins. Well, therefore, may we go to him with the contrition of the prodigal in our hearts, and his confession on our lips—Father, I have sinned against heaven and in thy sight. The Spirit of God helping us thus to go to God, be assured that the father, who, seeing his son afar off, ran to meet him, fell on his neck, and kissed him, was but an image of Him, who, not sparing his own Son, but giving him up to death, that we might live, invites and now waits your coming.

THE FATHER.

The representations of God the Father in the most splendid paintings of the ancient masters are worse than in bad taste. His Son assumed the human form; and far short as the highest art comes of expressing the love and mildness and majesty that beamed in the face of Jesus, we are not offended by its efforts. Though they may not satisfy, they do not shock us. But to set forth the invisible God, in the character of the "Ancient of Days" as an old man, or even in the noblest aspects of humanity, is an irreverence—offensive and revolting.

Yet there have been representations of our heavenly Father more revolting. He has suffered less injustice from painters than from preachers. Thundering out the terrors of the law, armed with bolts of vengeance, and scowling down from pulpits, they have stood there as unlike as possible to him who wept over Jerusalem, and when he saw the multitudes had compassion on them. By representing God in dark and gloomy colors, with an expression on his countenance of stern severity, and as more prone to punish than to pardon, the preacher's offence is greater than the painter's. He may quench a sinner's hopes, extinguish the light that is dawning on a darkened soul, and repel a poor prodigal whose steps are turning homeward to his father's house. A physician who kills the patient he should have cured, such a man is practically the enemy of souls; to use Paul's words, he destroys him for whom Christ died.

To such false and forbidding representations of the Father, what a contrast is the beautiful, most touching, affecting, winning portrait which we have here, from one who knows him well—from the hand of his own Son. This picture might kindle hope in the bosom of despair. Some have been afraid to present God in such a gracious light, lest men, taking encouragement to plunge headlong into sin, should, like this prodigal, depart from the living God. Depart from the living God? Ah, that is not to do! Like lost sheep we have all gone astray—all departed from him. But for one person who, abusing the grace of God, takes occasion from this parable to go on in sin, with the intention, when the worst comes to the worst, of returning to the arms of an indulgent Father, thousands have been saved by it from sinking into despair, and plunging into deeper guilt. Inspiring them with hope, it has raised many a poor wretch from the swine-troughs, and brought them home. Followers of the prodigal, they have gone in to sit down in the kingdom of heaven—the angels who rejoiced over them, now rejoicing with them. In contemplating this picture, see

HOW THE FATHER RECEIVED HIS SON.

When he was yet a great way off, it is said, his father saw him. How did that happen? I knew a sailor's widow who had parted with her husband after some brief, bright days of marriage. He went to sea and never came back; his ship, probably foundering with all her crew, was never more heard of. When the time expired for her return, but no ship came, this woman would repair to a rocky headland, and, looking out, watch every sail on the wide ocean in the hope, as some ever and anon made for the harbor, that each was his—bringing the lost one home. And at night, on her lone bed, she used to lie awake, listening to the footsteps of belated travellers, fancying that she recognized his step—but only, as the sound passed her door, to weep over her disappointment; and long after hope had died in the breasts of others, on rocky cliff or lonely bed she waited his coming who never, never came home.

Such love, I can fancy, often led this father's steps to some rising ground, where others knowing his purpose but appearing not to notice him, he repaired; and, with a heart yearning for his son, turned his eyes in the direction the prodigal went off, hoping to see him return. One day when on his watch-post, he descries a new object in the distance. He watches it. It moves; it advances; it is not a beast, prowling lion, or hungry wolf; it is a man; it may be his son. His heart beats quick. One long, earnest, steadfast gaze, and, joy of joys, happy hour, often prayed for and come at last, the keen eye of love recognizes it—it is the prodigal come back! Painfully, for he was foot-sore and weary; slowly, for he bent under a load of guilt; sadly, for the scene around reminded him of departed joys and blighted innocence, his mother mouldering in her grave, and his father with gray hairs, he had almost, perhaps, brought down to his; tremblingly, for he was in doubt of his reception—with head hung down, and slow, halting, hesitating step, the prodigal comes on. Like one agitated by contending emotions, uncertain how to act, with what measure of indulgence to temper severity, does the father wait his son's approach? No. He does not stand on his dignity; nor say, Let him make the first advances, and ask forgiveness. His one thought is, This is my son, my poor son; his one feeling a gush of love; his only impulse to throw his arms around his child, and clasp him to a bosom that has never ceased to love and hope for his return. As soon, therefore, as the wanderer is recognized, on flying feet the old man runs to meet him; and ere the son has time to speak a word, the father has him in his arms, presses him to his bosom, and, covering his cheek with passionate kisses, lifts up his voice and weeps for joy.

And this is God! the God whom we preach, as he is drawn by the hand and seen in the face of Him whom he sent to seek and save us, to bring us back, to open a way of reconciliation—the God whose Spirit inspires us with our first feeble desires to return—the God who, unwilling that any should perish, invites and waits our coming. "Therefore," like that father, often looking out for his son, "will the Lord wait, that he may be gracious unto you, and therefore," as was fulfilled by Jesus on his cross, "will he be exalted, that he may have mercy upon you. Blessed are all they that wait for him: The people shall dwell in Zion; thou shalt weep no more. He will be very gracious unto thee at the voice of thy cry: when he shall hear it, he will answer thee."

HOW HIS FATHER TREATED THE PRODIGAL.

"The king kissed Absalom"—an act that here as there expressed more than mere affection. As in David's palace, where Absalom was brought back after years of banishment, and his crimes were forgiven by a father who, all the time his face was turned from his wicked son, had, as Joab perceived and the Bible says, his heart toward him, the kiss here is a sign of reconciliation—a pledge that the past is all forgiven. Forgiven, but deeply penitent; sorrowful, yet rejoicing; happy with his father, but more than ever vexed with himself that he should have wronged and injured him, the prodigal is conducted home. The tidings spread like wild-fire; the house is moved; the servants hurry to the scene; and the joyful father issues orders that teach them, and reassure his son, that the long-lost one is to be reinstated in all the privileges which his crimes had forfeited.

Bring forth the fairest robe and put it on him, says the father. It is done; and, the rags of the swine-herd stript off, the best robe in the house is thrown over his naked shoulders, and flows in rich beauty to his bleeding feet; and there now he stands—a beautiful type of the investiture of a sinner in the righteousness and imputed merits of the Saviour—that best robe in God's own house, a garment

"Fairer than ever angel wore."

Put a ring, says the father next, on his finger. And what to him was an unexpected honor, is to us, since rings were used of old as seals, a type of those graces whereby the Holy Spirit seals believers unto the day of redemption. That ring, as the diamond on its golden hoop flashes with many colors, may have other meanings; signifying here the espousals between Christ and his Church, it may be the token of her marriage, the passport of those who are blessed to go in to the marriage-supper of the Lamb. Put shoes on his feet, says the father next,—a command that indicates more than a tender regard for him, whose bare, bleeding feet touch his father's heart. In these days, the servants and slaves wore no shoes, and were thus distinguished from the members of the family. The naked foot was a sign of servitude. This order, meant for more than his son's comfort and a covering to those wayworn feet, was therefore tantamount to a declaration from the father's lips that the prodigal was not to be regarded as a servant, but as a son; that to him belonged all the privileges and possessions of sonship; that he who had never lost his place in the father's heart, was now to resume it at his table and in his house.

Nor is this all—"Kill the fatted calf, and let us eat and be merry: for this my son was dead and is alive again; he was lost, and is found." He shall be feasted. As these hollow eyes and sunken cheeks and wasted form bear witness, he has starved long; but he shall be filled now. So the board is spread, the wine-cup circles, joy abounds, pleasure beams from every face, music shakes the air, and dancers' feet the floor; and there is more joy in that house over the lost one than over the one that was never lost. Poor prodigal! he needed it—" Give strong drink unto him that is ready to perish, and wine unto those that be of heavy hearts." Thus some of the greatest sinners, on being converted, have experienced a joy and peace and sense of divine love with which others were never blessed—even as a poor child, that has been brought down to the gates of death, receives the richest food, the sweetest cordials, and the tenderest nursing; hence the prayer which God delights to answer—

> "According as the days have been
> Wherein we grief have had,
> And years wherein we ill have seen,
> So do thou make us glad."

And this is God, Christ's Father and ours! Who, says David, shall not fear thee, O Lord! How may we, as we contemplate this picture, alter the words, saying, Who will not love thee, O Lord?—all the more when we remember, that while it cost that father nothing to save and receive his son, we were bought with a price. With what a price! The story of redemption is written in blood; God having sent his only begotten and beloved Son to the far country, to become a bondsman to set us free—to suffer and to die for us. Ring and robe, feast and fatted calf, the sound of music, and the sight of dancers, as the scene swims before the prodigal's eyes, convey to him the happy assurance of a father's love; yet how far inferior that evidence to the bleeding form that hung and groaned and died on Calvary! Love beyond parables and all images to express! God so loved the world, that he gave his only-begotten Son, that whosoever believeth in him might not perish, but have everlasting life!

HOW HIS FATHER REJOICED OVER THE PRODIGAL.

In Iceland are some springs called Geysers. Hot, and rising from basin-shaped fountains, they present very remarkable appearances. Like the tides of ocean, they have their ebb and flow. The water now flies from the spectator; and shunning the light, leaves its basin to bury itself in the bowels of the earth—nor gives any intimation of its existence but an occasional groan, a low, deep moaning. At the flow, which alternates with the ebb, it rises in its funnel, overflows its margin, and, with noises like salvos of artillery, sends up, amid clouds of snow-white vapor, a flashing, liquid column as high as a hundred feet.

So act the passions of joy and sorrow. Grief retires from observation. Hiding herself, she conceals rather than proclaims the sorrows that she feeds on; and as the stricken deer leaves the herd, the bereaved court retirement that they may weep in secret over their bleeding wounds. It is otherwise with joy. The Greek on making a discovery, of which he had long been in pursuit, was so transported, as to rush naked into the street, and, leading the people to believe him mad, cry, Eureka, Eureka—I have found it, I have found it! Joy must have vent. A fountain which not only flows but overflows, it bursts up and out, seeking to communicate its own happiness to others.

Thus some have been moved to proclaim their conversion, and tell others of the peace which they enjoyed in believing. Come all ye that fear the Lord, says the Psalmist, and I will tell what he hath done for my soul; and it is just as natural for a heart full of happiness and God's love to do that, as for a thrush, perched in a summer evening on the top of a cherry-tree, to pour out the joy that fills its little breast in strains of melody. It is the great President Edwards, I think, who relates how, on one occasion, he had such a sense of God's love, that he could hardly resist telling it to the woods, the flowers beneath his feet, and the skies above his head. No wonder, therefore, that when the pure and powerful joys of salvation are poured into a heart which sin had weakened, and never satisfied, the new wine should burst the old bottle,—flowing forth in what seems to those who know no better, but ostentation and parade. It is not so. Out of the fullness of the heart the mouth speaketh.

In this parable, so true in all its parts to nature, this feature of joy stands beautifully out. To these servants the father had never told his grief; but now the prodigal is come back, and his heart is bursting with joy, he tells them of it. He cannot conceal it. He does not seek to conceal it. He says, let us eat and be merry—I am so happy myself, I wish all others to be happy. Banish all care; drop your toils; let the shepherd come from the hill, the plowman from the furrow, the herd from the pastures, the meanest servant come; and all wearing smiles and joining in the song, hold holiday with my heart. My son that was dead is alive again; that was lost, is found. And this happiest of fathers, rejoicing over the returned prodigal, blotting out of memory all his offences, doating on him, drawing him to his side, clasping him in his arms, ever and anon bending on him looks of deepest love, pleading his cause with his unamiable brother, saying, It was meet that we should be merry, —is Christ's picture of his Father!—so he rejoices over every repenting, returning sinner.

Who that elder brother stands for, it is not so easy to settle—whether for Jews jealous of the Gentiles receiving an equal share with them of the blessings of grace; or, still more likely, for the Pharisees, who, proud of their ceremonial righteousness, regarded themselves as injured by the favor shown to publicans and sinners. Proud and boastful, heartless, selfish and sulky, he makes an excellent background to the picture—bringing out into striking prominence the kindness of the father's heart. That is man's heart—turned by sin and selfishness into a stone; this is God's. Is there no kind Christian father or mother, did they, on a wild winter night, when the heavens were black with drift, and flocks were perishing on the hill, and ships were sinking in the sea, and travellers were lost on the pathless moor, hear a prodigal child knocking at their door, and with wailing, sinking, dying voice, crying, Open and let me in! but would rise—ay, would spring to the call? They know how ready God is to receive every poor sinner to his mercy, and poor penitent to his bosom. He rejoices in his ransomed; let them rejoice in him! Rejoice in the Lord, says Paul, alway, and again I say, rejoice. The sun that shines on you shall set, and summer streams shall freeze, and deepest wells go dry—but not his love. His love is a stream that never freezes, a fountain that never fails, a sun that never sets in night, a shield that never breaks in fight; whom he loveth, he loveth to the end.

Are any alarmed lest such a picture of God as we have attempted to draw from this parable, should lead penitents to think lightly of sin? There is no ground for alarm. God forgives offences; but the forgiven never forget them. Does the prodigal forget his sins so soon as they are forgiven—freely, readily, kindly forgiven? No. On the contrary, though now assured of his father's love, he drops out all mention of a servant's place, he confesses and deplores his sins —does that when he knows them to be forgiven. A sense of God's kindness is the spring of deepest sorrow; and the repentance that succeeds forgiveness is truer and deeper than any which precedes it. Therefore when God says, "I will establish with thee an everlasting covenant," he adds, "*then* shalt thou remember thy ways, and be ashamed." It was when Jesus, whom Peter had denied, turned a look of love and pity on him, that Simon, pierced to the heart, went out to weep bitterly. The repentance that needeth not to be repented of, has its truest emblem in the rivers that, lending flowers and emerald verdure to their banks, wind through the valleys of the Alps. It is not when stern winter howls, but in spring, and the sweet summer-time, when birds are singing, and flowers are breathing odors, and the sun, from azure skies, pours down his beams on the icy bosoms of the mountains, that the rivers, fed by melted snows, rising and overflowing all their banks, roll their mightiest torrents to the lakes. And so it is when a sense of God's love, and peace, and forgiveness is poured into our hearts, that they thaw, and soften, and melt into streams of fullest sorrow. "They shall look on him whom they have pierced; and mourn as one mourneth for an only son, and be in bitterness, as one is in bitterness for a first-born."

IV.

The Parable of the Good Samaritan.

Luke x. 30—37.

ON those summer mornings, when dews—sowing, as Milton says, the earth with orient pearl—lie thick on the meadow, and hang the trees with diamonds, and the smoke from cottage chimneys rises through the still air in blue and wreathed and graceful columns, the water of a lake looks like a mirror for Nature to admire her beauty in; cloud and mountain, rocks and hanging woods, the cattle that pasture and the flowers that adorn the banks, all faithfully reflected in this beautiful image of a soul at peace. On such an occasion, let a stone be thrown far out into the bosom of the quiet waters, and so soon as it goes down with a sullen plunge, a wave rises. This assumes the form of a circle, and, widening out equally on all sides, extends itself to embrace a larger and larger sphere. Symbol of our love, such it should be.

To love all in an equal degree is indeed impossible, because though some have larger hearts than others, the affections, like our other powers, act within certain limits. Our understanding is confined within bounds that it cannot pass; many subjects lie beyond its reach. Our eyes have a limited range of vision; we see the stars, not those who inhabit them. Our ears have a still more limited range of hearing; we see the flash of lightning when, too distant on the horizon or in the upper regions of air for us to hear the thunder, no sound reaches us. On the other hand, God embraces all creatures—those which are farthest removed from him, as well as the lofty archangels that stand nearest his throne. His heart has room enough to hold them all. Infinite, not less than eternal and unchangeable, unaffected by space or place, knowing neither distance nor nearness, he embraces this world with all its creatures, and all other worlds with theirs, in his heart, as he embraces them all in his arms. But though we were originally made after his image, our affections are of limited capacity. They diminish in strength in proportion as the objects we love are removed from us—as the circle in the lake, the larger it grows in size grows the less in height, till it is lost in the distant waters, or dies with a feeble ripple on the shore. It cannot be otherwise, else we were gods, not men.

We must admit this, and that, as a candle, shining brighter on near than remote objects, gives more light to the room where it burns than to the traveller who sees it gleaming afar in the cottage window, our love necessarily grows weaker the more it is diffused. Still, like light, or the circle in the water, it ought, not moving in one direction rather than in another, nor limited in its outgoings to our own party, or sect, or race, or country, to diffuse itself on all around. Such is the grand and most necessary lesson which the parable of the Good Samaritan was designed to teach. In considering it, let us attend to

ITS OCCASION.

The Jews had no class whose office corresponded exactly to that of Christian ministers. But in their synagogues, where they met Sabbath by Sabbath to worship, and hear the Word of God enforced and explained, they had assemblies which corresponded more or less with our churches. There, after a fashion now only found among some Baptists and the Society of Friends, the public speaking was not engrossed by the leaders; but any person had the opportunity—which our Lord sometimes embraced—of addressing the congregation. Still, there was a class among the Jews who made the Bible their peculiar study; and who were therefore regarded as authorities on all questions connected with the laws of Moses. These men, the divines as we might call them and probably the common preachers of the country, were therefore called lawyers; and to the question of a man of that class, the world and church owe this beautiful parable.

The Evangelist says that he stood up and *tempted* our Lord, saying, Master, what shall I do to inherit eternal life? But we should do this lawyer injustice, and violate the charity which, thinking no evil, puts a favorable rather than an unfavorable construction on other men's conduct, were we to rank him with those who sought by their question about tribute to entrap our Lord. No doubt the same word is used in both instances. But to *tempt*—as when it is said that God tempted Israel, which in a bad sense we know he could not do—is simply to *try;* and by the law of charity, as well as from a regard to his answers and whole bearing, this man is entitled to a favorable construction both of his motives and object. He had heard of him whose fame filled the whole land; and to ascertain whether he was as great a teacher as fame, prone to exaggerate, reported, to measure his ability, perhaps to try his soundness, he tested him by this fair and momentous question: "Master, what shall I do to inherit eternal life?" It involved a weighty matter; and would God that all of us went to Jesus with the same question but with a still higher object—anxious and eager to be saved.

The words *do* and *inherit* which the lawyer employed, make it probable that there was such confusion in his ideas of the method of salvation as we find among many whose ignorance is less excusable. They seem to think that salvation is half of God's mercy and half of their own merits; that they are to do something, by way of reconciling themselves to an offended God, Christ doing the rest; his merits supplementing their shortcomings. Their prayers and pains, their good conduct and efforts after a holy life, though not sufficient to save them, are to fit them for being saved by the blood of Jesus. Now, how did our Lord meet such a case? As he treated Peter's—humbling his pride by bidding him walk the sea. The disciple who would have lorded it over his fellows, and claimed among them such pre-eminence as Popery has since given him in the Church, steps proudly on the billows; but has hardly left the boat's side, when, turning pale at the sight of the crested waves, he begins to sink. He confessed himself unequal to the ambitious task—crying, Lord, save me; I perish. It was such a course that our Lord followed here; and also on another such occasion. He bids this lawyer try the law; keep it if he can; obtain eternal life through obedience,—just to teach him, or rather to make his own failures teach him, that he cannot. When, in reply to Christ's question, he has recited the sum of the ten commandments, and shown, to his credit be it admitted, that he was acquainted with the spirit as well as the letter of the law, Jesus said to him, "Thou hast answered right: this do, and thou shalt live."

Whether there was anything in our Lord's tone or eye which, while his lips said, "Thou hast answered right: this do and live," said as plainly as words, You have not done it, and know you have not done it,—I do not know. But his own conscience smote the lawyer—telling him that what it was necessary and right to do, he had not done. To whatever extent he might deceive himself as to his loving God, he knew and remembered—as we all do—many cases in which he had not loved his neighbor as he loved himself. Well had it been for him had he instantly thrown himself at the feet of Jesus, to cry, "Save me; I perish!" And well for us, if convincing us of sin and misery, and teaching us our inability to obtain salvation by its works, the law has been a schoolmaster to bring us to Christ. These words, "This do, and thou shalt live," certainly shut us all up to Christ. Too blind to see this, or too proud to acknowledge it, the lawyer, driven to his shifts, attempts to escape from the dilemma in which he finds himself. One door seems open—offering him escape. If he can confine the term neighbor within very narrow limits, he may evade the difficulty, and, though he had failed doing to many what he would have wished them to do to him, satisfy himself that he had kept the whole law. So, hoping to escape by this door—as Luke says, "willing to justify himself"—he immediately replied: "And who is my neighbor?"—a question that our Lord answers by a story, which, launching out beyond its limits, illustrates, in her active and true benevolence, the queen of graces—Christian Love. Let us attend now to the story of the Good Samaritan, as it divides itself into three distinct parts.

THE FIRST ACT.

The curtain rises to show a district of country lying between Jerusalem and Jericho. It is wild and rocky; a savage place—whose mountain caves conceal men, savage as the scenes they haunt. When one reads what crimes of violence and robbery were, less than a century ago, committed on travellers in the immediate neighborhood of London, and remembers how in their early days the mails were conveyed along the highroads by guards carrying fire-arms, we cease to wonder that the road between two such towns as Jericho and Jerusalem was infested by bold and bloody robbers. Between these two large cities there was, of course, much correspondence. Men of wealth and means often travelled the road—offering amid these wild and rocky solitudes a good chance for plunder; and where the carcase was, in outcasts, desperate men, and roving Bedouins, the eagles were gathered together. The gospel narrative represents this road as dangerous; and since some are now getting up objections to the Bible, which they are ignorant enough to fancy new—though they be as old as Tom Paine, and vain enough to deem unanswerable—though, answered over and over again, to refute them be to slay the slain, it may be worth while here to mark the perfect harmony between sacred and common history. Now, to say nothing of other authors, Josephus—the Jewish historian and no Christian, mentions that that road was in his day infested by robbers. It was the scene of such crimes as to be called, The Bloody Way; and so dangerous had it become to travellers, that Jerome states that the Romans found it necessary to erect a fort there for their protection.

Now, it is somewhere among its rocky defiles that the scene of this tragedy is laid. A solitary man appears—travelling from Jerusalem; from which it is said he went *down* to Jericho, just as we speak of going *up* to London, or coming *down* from it, because it is in point of fact our capital. Issuing from one of the defiles, or springing up from behind some rock, a band of ruffians fall on him. Very probably he stands on his defence. Swords are drawn; blows are struck; overpowered at length by superior numbers, he is felled to the ground. With all haste they plunder his person, nor stop till they strip him naked; and parting with a blow or two to finish their work, on the rule that dead men tell no tales, they hurry off—leaving him on the ground, insensible, helpless, dying, in a pool of blood. So the first act closes, and the curtain falls.

SECOND ACT.

The curtain rises on the same scene—the man is where he fell, the pool of blood growing larger as life ebbs away. But he is not alone now. Two new characters appear on the road, travellers also going down from Jerusalem to Jericho. The foremost is a priest; the second we might call a priest's assistant—a Levite. He also is a minister of religion, and an official of the temple. Here again mark the correspondence between this story and what we know from other sources to be well-attested facts. Judging by these, the priest and Levite are the very men we would have expected to appear. The Jewish priests, though their homes were scattered over the country, were required, somewhat as the canons do in English cathedrals, to serve by turns in the temple at Jerusalem; and since no fewer than twelve thousand priests and Levites had their ordinary residence in Jericho, you will see how often they must have travelled this road, and how natural therefore their appearance on the scene.

Ministers of religion, fresh from the service of the holy sanctuary, men to whom others looked for an example of all that was humane, magnanimous, and godlike, in them surely help was at hand! It seemed a happy fortune for this unfortunate man that countrymen, strangers neither in faith nor speech nor blood; men devoted to duties calculated not to harden but to soften the heart; not to secularize and lower, but to improve and elevate the mind, and to form, in short, a noble character—should be the first to find him. Alas! this poor, bleeding victim may live or die for them. First the one, and then the other approaches —the Levite making a closer inspection than the priest. What then? No sooner do they see his naked form bleeding to death on the ground, than instead of hasting to his aid, shouting for help, and doing their utmost to save him, both pass on the other side; and, pressing forward, leave him to his miserable fate. David says, Put not your trust in princes; nor—says this story, and many portions of history besides—in priests.

Not that some excuse may not be pleaded for the priest and Levite. Not long years ago, in some cities of fair and sunny Italy, if a man was assassinated in broad day, and on the public streets, people fled the scene, leaving the wretch to die, lest, found by the bloody corpse, they should be accused of the murder. Such might be the fears which moved these men to what seemed a cruel neglect. Besides, it is plain that they themselves were in some danger of sharing a similar fate. The ship steers wide of the rock on which another lies wrecked. Its inhabitants fly from a house on fire—consulting their own safety, and thinking more how they themselves shall escape the danger, than how they may save others from it. And naturally enough supposing that these rocks, in the perpetrators of this bloody deed, concealed men who waited to repeat it on the next passenger, they only did what thousands would have done—when, leaving this poor wretch to his fate, they hurried from the scene. Besides, his case seemed hopeless. To attempt to save him, therefore, was only to waste time, and rashly expose themselves—to risk their own lives without any great probability of being able to save his. Then they had this flattering unction to lay to their souls, that they had not done this wrong; his blood was not on their hands: neither their friend, nor brother, nor acquaintance, he had no special claim on them. It was other people's business as much as theirs to aid him. What was he to them, or they to him?

I do not say that these were good excuses. Still, they are as good, and better than many have to offer, who, passing by misery on the other side, indulge a hateful selfishness—heaping up riches at the expense of the poor and needy, to the neglect of such as are ready to perish. God forbid that I should even seem to justify this priest and Levite! "With them, mine honor, be not thou united!" Yet there are thousands who have no right to condemn them. Condemning them, we are happy if we do not condemn ourselves. The same spirit of hateful and ungodly selfishness still walks the world; and, though in less tragic circumstances, how often have I encountered it—wearing a new face, perhaps a fair mask, but the same old enemy of God and man? The Jewish economy is gone; its temple is a ruin; its priests and Levites have passed from the stage of time—but not that selfish spirit. It belongs to our fallen nature. Nor will it ever be eradicated till God pour out his Spirit upon all flesh, and Christian love, in millennial days, reigns over a regenerated world, and crime and selfishness, if not all suffering, banished from earth, the golden rule shall be universally owned and acted on—"Do unto others as ye would have others do unto you." Even so come, Lord Jesus! Come quickly!

THIRD ACT.

This story recalls another which I could not read without mingled feelings of anger and admiration. Dismasted and waterlogged on the wide ocean, a thousand miles away from the nearest land, a bark had drifted about till all hope of relief was dead in her starving crew. The cry, a ship! a ship! roused their flagging energies. Shawl and shirt on the end of boat-hooks were waved as signals of distress. The stranger changed her course and bore down on the miserable wreck. They put forth their utmost strength to send a long, loud shout over the deep: and as, on her nearing them, they discovered their country's flag, they congratulated each other on being saved. Who can fancy what men felt who had been for days hanging over a horrible death, at this blessed change? But still less can we fancy the sudden revulsion of feeling, the terrible sinking of heart, the awful howl which rose to heaven, when the other vessel, sailing near enough to see the ghastly wretches who implored their pity, put about, and, going off on the other tack, left them to despair. Nor was that all. Recalling that scene in the infernal torments of the heathen poet, where Tantalus fills the cup, and no sooner raises it to his thirsty lips, than the water vanishes, the same hopes had been raised before by another ship—manned also by their countrymen, to suffer the same cruel disappointment. Sometimes cold and thin, blood, as their rescue proved, is not always thicker than water. When death had seized some, and despair all, a Norwegian bark, by God's good providence, came sailing across their path. Pity filled the hearts and eyes of the foreign sailors; nor till they had carried the last survivor on board their ship, did they desert the wreck, and leave it to drift away over the ocean—a wandering coffin with its unburied dead. A noble act! but still nobler his who now appears on the scene of this bloody tragedy to redeem the character of humanity, become an exemplar, in Christ's hands, to all future ages, and gaining an immortal renown, win for himself the famous title of The Good Samaritan. To appreciate his conduct aright, let us consider

WHO HE WAS.

He was "a certain Samaritan," is all that we are told. His name has not been preserved. No matter— he has left a broad footprint on the sands of time : and we may hope that, like many more nameless ones, his memorial is in the "book of remembrance" of which Micah speaks, saying, "They shall be mine, saith the Lord, in that day when I make up my jewels; and I

will spare them as a man spareth his son that serveth him." On him, as a Samaritan, the wounded man has no claim; they are not countrymen—one either in blood or faith. The Samaritans were not, as some suppose, a race of degenerate Jews, with the blood of Abraham, though adulterated by admixture, flowing in their veins. When the land that had been occupied by the ten tribes was cleared, and they were carried away into perpetual captivity, their place was supplied thus: "The King of Assyria brought men from Babylon, and from Cuthah, and from Ava, and from Hamoth, and from Sepharvaim, and placed them in the cities of Samaria instead of the children of Israel: and they possessed Samaria, and dwelt in the cities thereof." Heathen colonists, they brought their gods with them; and though, with the view of being delivered from the lions, which, multiplying rapidly while the country lay waste, disputed possession of it with the new settlers, they adopted some Jewish forms, and stood in some awe of him they counted the God of the land, they clung long by their old faith. It is said of them in the book of Kings, what is remarkably descriptive of many professing Christians, "they feared the Lord, and served their own gods." Being enlightened in the course of time by the truth which streamed in on them from the Jews, whose territories surrounded theirs, the Samaritans came at last to abandon the faith and practices of their heathen fathers. Setting up a temple and worship in Samaria, in opposition to that which had its seat in Jerusalem, they became worshipers of the true God.

They had ceased to be heathens; still they were heretics. For, though they admitted the divine authority of the first five Books of Moses, they utterly rejected the Psalms, the prophets, and all the remaining portions of the Bible. For these reasons the Jews hated them—their rivalry, their heresy, and their heathen blood, breeding a bitterly rancorous hatred. So strong was this antipathy, that the woman by Jacob's well was astonished that our Lord would ask of her even a drink of water, saying, How is it that thou, being a Jew, askest drink of me, which am a woman of Samaria? for, adds the evangelist, "the Jews have no dealings with the Samaritans." Refusing them the common civilities of life, they used their name as a term of the bitterest reproach—for everything that was bad and abhorrent. When his enemies, for example, were so transported with rage against our Lord that forgetting the sacredness of the place, they rose up in the temple to stone him, their passions found vent in this speech as the very concentration of the fiercest hatred: "Say we not well," they cried, as they gnashed their teeth on him, "Say we not well, that thou art a *Samaritan*, and hast a devil?"

It was to one of this race that the priest and Levite left their wounded countryman. Many a bitter gibe and sneer had this Samaritan suffered of the Jews; but now with that wretched man in his hands his hour of vengeance had arrived—and nobly he avenged himself! Alone with the victim,—no eye on him but the vulture's that, perched on a rock, waited the close of life's struggle to descend with foul beak and flapping wing on its prey,—he approaches, and bends over the dying man; but not to finish what the robbers had all but completed. Risking his property, venturing even his life, he treats a fallen enemy as if he had been a wounded brother—his own mother's son. How beautiful is humanity!

And how hateful the antipathies over which love won this signal triumph! Hateful in the Jew, they are, whether connected with churches, sects, nations, races, or colors, doubly hateful in the Christian—the follower of the meek and lowly and loving Jesus, of him in whom there is neither Jew nor Greek, bond nor free. Yet see how the laws of humanity and Christian love are outraged by the antipathy which the white man bears to the patient and injured African! In America, for instance, color is worse than a crime. The Bible declares that God has made of one blood all nations of the earth, and by one blood redeemed them; and in practical contempt both of God and his word, they refuse to eat at the same table, ride in the same carriage, worship in the same church, or, unless under the pressure of a dire necessity, even to fight in the same ranks with the negro; it is the old story,—" the Jews have no dealings with the Samaritans."

Here are the old, bad human passions. What if time should bring round as remarkable a parallel in God's righteous and retributive providences? Those whom one age sees riding on the top of the wheel of fortune, the next often sees eating dust. The fate of nations, as of individuals, has not seldom illustrated the laws expressed in these sayings: Pride goeth before destruction; The fathers have eaten sour grapes, and the children's teeth are set on edge. May those who have enslaved the unhappy negroes, bought and sold their brethren like cattle, trampled them under foot, and, using their name also as a term of reproach, repudiated something more sacred than their State debts—the claims of a common parentage and a common redemption—take warning! The haughty, intolerant, contemptuous Jews would not hear the warning, "Woe to the crown of pride!" and now they are a by-word, a proverb, and a hissing,—a nation scattered and peeled. As ages roll on, the providence of God will continue to show that it is not war with its bloody triumphs, nor commerce with its wealth, nor science with its arts, but righteousness that exalteth a nation. Depend on it, that the bread we cast on the waters, whether for evil or for good, will return, though after many days. There is one true policy for nations and individuals. Regardless of immediate consequences, let them do what is right; if they have done wrong repent it, and, if possible, repair it—this their rule: What doth the Lord require of thee? but to do justly, and love mercy, and walk humbly with thy God.

WHAT THE SAMARITAN DID.

So soon as he saw the man weltering in his blood, it is said, "he had compassion on him." So, perhaps, had the priest and Levite. But observe, no mention is made of that; no account is kept of it, any more than we keep account of the blossoms in the orchard that come to nothing—are beautiful, but nipped by late frosts or blown away by winds, never turn to fruit. In that respect, this book is an exemplar of another, the book of judgment. It is deeds only that are entered there. "I was an hungered, and ye gave me meat; I was thirsty, and ye gave me drink; I was a stranger, and ye took me in; naked, and ye clothed me; I was sick, and ye visited me; I was in prison, and ye came unto me." "Go and *do* thou likewise."

Now what did the Samaritan do? Conquering his prejudices, and those fears for his safety which amid such scenes and with such a sight before him were not unnatural, he hastes to the rescue. Throwing himself from his steed, he bends over the bleeding form, and finding life still there, applies such remedies as circumstances permitted and his skill suggested. It was and is still common in the East, for travellers to carry their provisions with them; and it providentially happened here that what the Samaritan had for eating was not unsuitable for healing—the one man's meat was fit to be the other man's medicine. For that purpose he uses it—esteeming it better that he should suffer hunger than that this poor wretch should suffer death. Nor in oil and wine were his applications so unsuitable, and his surgery so rude, as some might fancy. In ancient times oil was employed to mollify wounds and deaden their pain; and wine to stanch their bleeding; and Galen, one of the greatest of Roman physicians, pronounces them excellent means for such ends. They were at any rate the best he had. Like the woman in the gospel, he did what he could—

pouring them into the wounds, which he hastily tore his own robes to bind. And as he watched with eager interest the signs of returning life, I can fancy the joy that thrilled through all his frame, when the pulse began again to beat, and color returned to the bloodless cheek, and, opening his eyes, this poor man fixed them with looks of eloquent gratitude on the face of his kind benefactor.

Some, on beginning a good work, go at it at first with zeal; but lacking perseverance, and loving change, they soon turn to something else—tiring of it, as children of their toys. But the Samaritan stuck by the cause on which he had embarked; and so presents an humble illustration of him who will perfect that which concèrneth his people, and wherever he begins a good work carry it on to the day of the Lord Jesus. Tenderly lifting up the wounded, he places him on his own beast, and conveys him to an inn, which he (type as we shall see of our Lord) approaches in the form of a servant—walking while the other rides. In these countries no other accommodation was commonly provided for travellers than what the caravanserais still offer in bare walls and the shelter of a roof; but here the inn was one of the few which, anticipating our modern civilization, in landlord and other provisions resembled our own.

Having ventured his life to save the Jew, and plucked him, I may say, from the wreck, bringing him safe to shore, the Samaritan's work was in a sense done. As the prophet said to the Shunamite, when, having called her boy back to life, he laid him in her happy arms, saying, "Woman, behold thy son," my work is done, it is yours now to care for him,—so he, casting the poor Jew on the kindness of his countrymen, might have left him; and had done so crowned with the highest honors of humanity. But he does more. He will finish what he has so well begun. Business calls him away next morning, but before leaving he undertakes all the expenses of this man's board and cure. "Twopence," the sum he left with the host, may seem to us inadequate; but money then had a different value from what it has now—a single penny being a good day's wages for a good day's work. Moreover, wise as he was humane, provident as he was generous—qualities that commonly shine in conjunction like binary stars, the Samaritan undertook, in case the sum should fall short, to make good the deficiency when he next came that way. So, earning the admiration of the inn, and followed by the blessings of the wounded man, bringing a blush, let us hope, to the cheek of priest and Levite, and winning for himself an imperishable renown, this most noble philanthropist went on his way—his purse lighter, but his heart happier; in one sense poorer, but in another richer; finding a fame he never sought; and little dreaming of the finger that pointed the eyes of the world to his example, or the voice that said in words which shall ring, in never-dying echoes, on its ear, Go, and do thou likewise.

"Go, and do thou likewise"—this is the moral of the story. It was told to rebuke the narrow-minded prejudices and selfishness of the Jews. May it rebuke our own! Our love is confined within narrow channels, because it is a tiny stream. Let it swell into a bigger volume, and these could not contain it; and therefore may God, pouring out his Spirit in showers from heaven, so flood our hearts with love, that it shall burst the boundaries within which education, ecclesiastical or national prejudices confine it, and, burying, drowning them, flow forth to all mankind! By this story Jesus teaches us to do good to all men as we have opportunity, and to rejoice in the opportunities of doing it. If any man's sorrows need our sympathy, his bodily or spiritual wants our help, let us think no more of asking whether he belongs to our country or family, our party or church, than if we saw him stretching out his hands from the window of a burning house, or found him, like this object of the Samaritan's kindness, expiring in a pool of blood. Thus Christ loved us; and thus he teaches us to love one another. This leads me to remark, in bringing these observations to a close, that

JESUS CHRIST HIMSELF WAS THE GOOD SAMARITAN.

To jaundiced eyes blushing rose, blue sky, and green earth, everything looks yellow; and so much does the appearance of objects depend on the medium through which we regard them, that viewed through stained glass, for instance, they assume its peculiar hue. Thus, if it is colored red, the gentle moon puts on a fierce and angry aspect; and as if, at the sounding of the second angel, the burning mountain of the Apocalypse were cast into the sea, its waters change to blood. Fancy, under the influence of our affection, plays us, if I may say so, such tricks—is equally illusive. Distempered by grief, the weeping mother, in sounds that startle only her, hears the pattering of her dead infant's feet. Looking through superstitious fears, the peasant sees a ghost in the tombstone which the moon, bursting from a cloud, suddenly whitens; and as the owl hoots from the gray steeple, or brushes past him on noiseless wing, he rushes in frantic terror from the quiet dwellings of the dead. The Romans, bringing to the invasion of our country, tender recollections of their own, on reaching the top of the hill which looks down on the Tay, exclaimed, Behold the Tiber! And under the influence of feelings stronger than fear, more sacred than grief, and loftier than patriotism, fancy has created resemblances and seen things in the Bible, that had no existence other than in a pious imagination. One example of that shines in a constellation of southern skies, and another blooms in the flowers of our conservatories. It was the reverence and love of Jesus Christ in the bosom of the ancient mariner, which, working through fancy, when his ship first plowed the waters of southern seas, saw suspended in the heavens, and formed of brilliant stars— and looking down on the world, the tree on which its Saviour hung; and it was the same piety that discovered in the passion-flower an imitation by the hand of nature of the instruments of our Redeemer's torture, and of the halo which now crowns his head in glory. And it is the same piety which, by a pardonable mistake, has in some instances discerned types, symbols, and shadows of Jesus in the Bible, that belong more to the regions of fancy than of fact.

It may be that in seeing Christ in this Good Samaritan, we have passed into this cloud-land; it may be that this is no more than a devout imagination. But the fancy does not, at any rate, pervert God's word from its grand purpose, nor in the pulpit prostitute to mean and common purposes a place that should be sacred to the saving doctrines of "Jesus Christ and him crucified." Here we rise, not sink; and as if we ascended on a sunbeam to its source in the sun itself, here we turn from contemplating Christian love in the Samaritan, to contemplate it in the Saviour—its celestial source and perfect pattern.

Viewed in this light, the story of the Good Samaritan grows in interest, and assumes the grandest character. The whole scene changes: and with it the characters that act their various parts upon the stage. Jerusalem, the city of the living God, with the mountains standing round about her, and crowned by the temple where Jehovah dwelt, now stands for man's originally happy and holy state. Man leaves it. He goes *down* from it; travelling downward to that place of misery, so aptly typified by that Jericho, against which the ark and armies of the living God waged war, and whose walls lay under this fatal shadow—"Cursed," said Joshua, as he stood on its smoking, blood-stained ruins, "cursed be the man before the Lord, that riseth up and buildeth this city Jericho; he shall lay the foundation thereof in his first-born, and in his youngest son shall he set up the gates of it." In the fierce and savage robbers, who issue from their haunts in this gloomy gorge to spring on the traveller, assault him, rob him, strip him, wound him, leaving him to die in his blood, we see the enemy of souls—the spoiler of Eden—the robber of man's innocence and happiness and honor—Satan, who was a murderer, says our Lord, from the beginning. In the priest and Levite, its fit, official representatives, the law comes with its works. But it does nothing for man—it can do nothing. These, its representatives who pass on the other side, and refuse even to own this wounded wretch, teach us, that "by the deeds of the law shall no flesh living be justified." The law has not the heart of mercy that takes compassion on the lost: nor in atoning merits oil and wine to stop the bleeding of sin's mortal wounds. These are brought to the scene, to the rescue, to save at the uttermost, by Him who painted his own portrait in the Good Samaritan. "What the law could not do, in that it was weak through the flesh, God sending his own Son in the likeness of sinful flesh, and for sin condemned sin in the flesh, that the righteousness of the law might be fulfilled in us who walk not after the flesh, but after the Spirit." There is balm in Gilead, and a physician there.

If that Good Samaritan was a figure of the God-man, Jesus Christ, would God the man he saved at death's door was a figure of us! May we be as willing as he to be saved! May we look to Jesus with the love that burned in his heart and beamed in his eyes! May we give ourselves as much over to Christ's care and cure, as he to his kind benefactor, when he lay in his arms, and hung helpless on his neck; and with still warmer gratitude than his, may we ever cherish in our very heart of hearts, the memory of this world's Good Samaritan!

V.

The Parable of the Unjust Judge.

Luke xviii. 1.

IN descending by one of the passes of the Alps into the lovely valley of the Saarnen, the traveller may notice on the right hand of the path a pine-tree, growing in extraordinary circumstances. Enormous masses of hoary rock lie scattered in the bottom of the ravine; they have fallen from the crags which form its stupendous walls; and it is on the top of one of these, a bare, naked block, that the pine-tree stands. No dwarf, misshapen thing, like the birch or mountain ash on an old castle wall, where the wind or passing bird had dropped the seed: it is a forest giant—with rugged trunk, and top that shoots, a green pyramid, to the skies. At first sight one wonders how a tree, seated on the summit of a huge stone, raised above the soil, with no apparent means of living, could live at all; still more, grow with such vigor as to defy the storms that sweep the pass, and the severe, long winters that reign over these lofty solitudes.

A nearer approach explains the mystery. Finding soil enough on the summit, where lichens had grown and decayed, to sustain its early age, it had thrown out roots which, while the top stretched itself up to the light, lowered themselves down the naked stone—feeling for the earth and food. Touching the ground at length, they buried themselves in it, to draw nourishment from its unseen, but inexhaustible, supplies to feed the feeble sapling into a giant tree. So we thought, as we stood looking on this natural wonder, the believer grows. Tempest-tossed by many storms, but, like the pine-tree with its gnarled roots grown into mighty cables, firmly moored to the Rock of Ages, he also raises his head to the skies, and through his prayers, draws spiritual nourishment and growth in grace from the inexhaustible supplies which lie hidden in Jesus Christ, and are provided for all such as love him. Often placed in circumstances not less unfavorable to his growth than that naked stone to the growth of the pine perched on its summit, his prayers, like the roots that descended to the soil, and penetrating it, brought up its riches to feed the tree, form a living communication between him and God. Thus his life is sustained: thus he grows in grace—green and fruitful where others wither, and living where others die. Such being the office of prayer, and the end it serves, it can surprise none to find one or two of our Lord's parables devoted to so great a duty: indeed, anything else would have surprised us on the part of Him who spent, not hours, but whole nights, in prayer. The sun, as it sank in the western sea, often left him, and as it rose behind the hills of Moab returned to find him on his knees.

In almost all our Lord's other parables, the truth which they are intended to teach is stated at their close. We travel through the story before we arrive at the moral. Here that meets us at the entrance, standing like an inscription over the door of a public building to tell its use and purpose, in these words: "He spake a parable unto them to this end, that men ought always to pray, and not to faint." As Matthew Henry says, "This parable has its key hanging at the door." Let us, however, take up the story first, and afterwards the persons it introduces in the order in which they appear.

THE UNJUST JUDGE.

Others besides judges may be unjust—the trustee who takes advantage of his position to defraud the widow or fatherless whom a dying friend has cast on his care; the merchant who, adulterating his goods, deceives his customers, or, removing them, defrauds his creditors; the tradesman who, earning the wages of iniquity, makes bad work pass for good. But these are not to be compared with an unjust judge. Of all men, he is the worst; unless, perhaps, the minister of religion, be he Bishop or Presbyter, who takes advantage of his position to disseminate error, or corrupt the morals of society. To such cases how appropriate the question—If the light that is in you be darkness, how great is that darkness! If the foundations be destroyed, what can the righteous do?

To pollute the fountains of justice is, indeed, one of the greatest evils which can be inflicted on society. It is like poisoning the public wells, or the air we breathe, or the bread we eat. Its inevitable result is anarchy. Denied justice by those who should dispense it, despairing of protection to life, liberty, and property, men will, as our forefathers did, take the law in their own hands—become, as the Apostle says, a law unto themselves; and, executing vengeance on the workers of iniquity, commit deeds which it is easier for us to condemn than it was for them to refrain from,—and which no man will harshly condemn who remembers these words of Scripture, "Surely oppression maketh a wise man mad."

This unjust judge recalls days when in England one of her greatest sons, the father of modern philosophy, and we trust, notwithstanding his error, a true Christian, Lord Bacon, was ignominiously dismissed from the bench for accepting a bribe; and when, in Scotland, scaffolds reeked with the best blood of the land, shed by iniquity on the seat of judgment. We ought not, and we cannot, recall those times without blessing God that, though not without the frailties that belong to humanity, our judges are just and our exactors righteous. It is certain that hundreds and thousands now living who have done no wrong would have been hanged in olden times; and, when expressing our loyalty to the heir of a throne that, amid the convulsions which shake other nations, stands secure in the affections of our own, let us cherish the memory of the mighty dead; and the gratitude we owe to the patriots who shed their blood to purify the fountains of public justice, and purchase the liberties of the people

—making our country the envy of the world. By them the Lord hath done great things for us whereof we are glad, and wherefore we should be grateful.

This parable turns on a state of public affairs of which we happily are ignorant; but it came home to the understanding of those whom our Lord addressed. The most common characteristic of Eastern nations was, and is still, the difficulty of clients obtaining justice. How astonished we should be if any judge, on retiring from the bench into private life, were to protest that he had never sold justice; never by accepting a bribe, stained the ermine of his robe! Yet a better man than they, or we, did so. In taking his leave of a people, some of whom, judging that noble old man by themselves, were mean enough to suspect him of mercenary ends, Samuel, indignant at the foul suspicion, said—"I am old and grayheaded; behold, here I am; witness against me before the Lord and before his anointed. Whose ox have I taken? or whose ass have I taken? or whom have I defrauded? whom have I oppressed, or of whose hand have I received any bribe to blind mine eyes therewith, and I will restore it?" It is a sorrowful thing to think that such a man should have had to stoop to this defence; but if calumny had breathed even on Samuel, dimming for a brief moment the lustre of his character, it shows how many unjust judges there were in old times, and how our Lord, in the picture of this one, was painting a very common portrait—as was his wont, drawing his illustrations of divine truth from familiar objects.

Now, in studying this picture of the Judge, let us look at

HIS CHARACTER.

A bold, bad man; he says—"I fear not God, nor regard man." What unblushing effrontery! yet in their autobiographies men are seldom so honest. His conduct corresponds to his character. Had he feared God, this widow had not waited so long on justice. "Ye shall not," said the Lord, "respect persons, in judgment; but ye shall hear the small as well as the great. Ye shall not be afraid of the face of man, for the judgment is God's."

A bold, bad man; he had no regard for the good opinion even of his fellow-men. Not that that morally qualifies a man for an office which he only is fit to fill who believes in the judgment of the oath which he administers, and that he who tries others, stripped of his state and placed at God's bar, shall himself one day be tried. An immoral life debauches the mind as well as the body—blunting the fine edge of conscience.

Nor, unless they are men of principle and of character, has a country any security that her judges will be just or her exactors righteous? Animated by the fear of God, a man will do right though all the world think him wrong; Pilate would have faced round on the Jewish crowd, and placing himself between Jesus and his enemies, seized a lull in the storm, to say, in answer to their cries of "Crucify, crucify him,"—He shall not be crucified; otherwise than over my dead body you shall not reach this innocent victim. The world, no doubt, has substitutes for the fear of God; and though in their nature inferior motives, a sense of honor, regard to the good opinion of mankind, the love of praise, and the fear of censure, are not without value. But even to these this judge was insensible, caring neither for God nor for man, so he gained his own selfish ends—got his appetites gratified, and enjoyed a life of ease and pleasure.

Let me remark that, in this hateful picture of selfishness incarnate, we see human nature, if I may say so, full blown; and in him, what all of us should be, were God to withhold the influences of his Spirit, or withdraw the restraints of his Providence. In yonder starved and beaten, caged and cowed animal of velvet step and painted skin, that but now and then shows its teeth to utter an angry growl, you do not see the tiger. Unchain him, uncage him; and there now is the bloody tyrant of the jungle, as with roar of thunder and eyes of fire, he leaps from his den, and with a blow of his paw felling one of the flying crowd, fastens on his throat to suck the flowing blood. And never is the sin inherent in our nature fully seen but in cases such as this, where, somehow or other, it grows up to its full development—fearless of God and regardless of man. Hence the necessity of being born again; and that we all should offer, and God to all of us should answer, the prayer of David, "Create in me a clean heart."

THE WIDOW.

Not long years ago you might have seen a pile of wood on the banks of the Ganges, surrounded by a mighty throng. The crowd opens, and up through the vista a lifeless body is carried to be laid on the summit of that funeral pile. Again the crowd opens, and, like a wave in the wake of a ship, it closes behind a woman, the dead man's widow, who comes to share his fiery bed. Attired for the sacrifice, on taking farewell of children and friends, she lies down by the corpse. As she embraces it in her arms the signal is given, and the pile is lighted; and, though in some instances, mad with agony and all on fire, the victim would leap for life through the flames and smoke, commonly, while her piercing shrieks were drowned in shouts, the poor widow submitted with patience to her fate. She submitted to it very much to escape a worse one. These funeral piles throw a lurid glare on the wretched state of widows in that heathen land; and, though not doomed in all other lands to so hard a fate, oppression and cruelty was the common lot of a class than which there is none that owes more to the humanizing influences of Christianity. I suppose there are few of us but, among competing claimants on our pity, time, money, help, would, whether she were a queen or beggar, give the preference to one in a widow's garb. Here we see the benign influence of the Gospel, and God fulfilling his words—"Let thy widows trust in me." How cruelly their circumstances were taken advantage of is plain from the manner in which God, constituting himself the husband of the widow, and espousing her cause, threatens to avenge her wrongs. Nor is this less evident, from the strong terms which our Lord employs to denounce those who, worst of hypocrites, made a stalking-horse of religion to get access to the widow's house, for the purpose of devouring her substance.

It is one of this class who demands justice from the unjust judge. None had less chance of getting it. Plundered probably of her little all, she has no money to buy it. Without powerful friends to back her, she has no means of compelling it. And to expect that this selfish, voluptuous, cold, iron-hearted man will espouse her cause, and put himself to trouble to see her righted, like a magnanimous judge—draw the sword of justice in her defence against the rich and the great, perhaps his own friends, alas! that were to run her horses on a rock, and plow there with oxen. Well may she renew her grief over a husband's grave; and as like a mother bird when the hawk is abroad, she gathers her little ones to her side, well may she clasp her hands to cry, God help me! there is none else to help. And yet from one who had no regard either to right or wrong, to whose eyes her distress brought no tears, and in whose heart her sorrows touched no chord of pity, she obtains justice—bringing fire out of a cold flint, gushing water from a hard, dry rock.—Consider

THE MEANS OF HER SUCCESS.

She owed it to importunity. Nature herself prompts to this—the babe cries till it gets a mother's breast. The power of importunity is one of the first lessons a child learns, and proceeds to practise. The boy keeps hanging on his father, harping on the same string, giving him no rest or peace, now pleading with winning smiles and now with tears, returning after every defeat to renew the attack, till, worn out, he yields assent; and thus by importunity, in a sense, the weak things of the world confound the mighty, and foolish things the wise. It is not long since it won daily triumphs in these streets, where the ragged boy, on naked feet, with piteous whine, and outstretched, emaciated hands, ran down the game. His story seemed to fall on a deaf ear; he knew better. Getting no answer but a rough refusal, he seemed to be wasting breath and time; he knew better. Following the object of his attentions like a shadow, sticking to him like a leech, robbing the day of its brightness, and the saunter of its pleasures, the urchin not only overcame the philanthropist's sense of the evils of indiscriminate charity, but opened even the niggard's hand. To get rid of a pest so intolerable, how often was he bought off with money?

This art is carried to its highest perfection in the East. A traveller in Persia tells how he was besieged by one who solicited a gift more costly than he was prepared to give. The hoary, and as the people esteemed him, holy mendicant set himself down before his gate, throwing up a rude tent to shelter himself from the noonday sun. There he remained like a sentinel; nor left his post but to follow the traveller out of doors, and return with him. Taking snatches of sleep during the day when the other rested in the house, he kept up a hideous howling and clamorous demands all the hours of night,—an annoyance which,

persisted in for successive days and nights, and even weeks, seldom failed, as you can suppose, to gain its object.

Such were the means by which the widow gained hers. So soon as ever this unjust judge took his seat at the gate of the city, where in the East courts are held and all causes heard, his eye as it roamed over the crowd fell on her. There she was, and always was— sorrow in her dress, but determination in the flash of her eye; her form bent down with grief, but her spirit unbroken; resolved to give that judge no rest till he had avenged her on her adversary. Now breaking in on the business of the court, she is on her feet passionately demanding justice; and now stretched on the ground at his, she piteously implores it. Nor can he shake her off. Denied her suit, she follows him to his house to interrupt his leisure and embitter his pleasures. Her voice ringing loud on the threshold demanding entry, she bursts into his presence; and is dragged away by the servants, thrust out, but only to return, as the ball struck rebounds—the billow shattered on the rock falls back into the deep to gather volume and strength for a new attack. And as by constant dashing the waves in time cut into the cliff, which, yielding to the incessant action of a weaker element, some day bows its proud head, and, precipitating itself forwards, falls into the sea, which swallowing it up, sweeps over it with jubilant, triumphant waves, so the persistence of the widow overcomes the resistance of the judge. Diamond cuts diamond. She conquers by importunity: yielding to her request, he says, " Because this widow troubleth me, I will avenge her, lest by her constant coming she weary me."

THE CONCLUSION,

Which our Lord draws, as expressed in the question, "Hear what the unjust judge saith; and shall not God avenge his own elect, which cry day and night unto him, though he bear long with them?"

There are points of resemblance between God's people and this widow. In Satan, have not we also an adversary to be avenged on? Are not we also poor and needy? She had known happy days; and so also had man. By death she had lost her husband; and by sin we have lost our God. Poor and friendless, she had no means of avenging, of righting herself; no more have we—we were without help when Christ died for the ungodly. "The sons of Zoruiah," cried David, "are too many for me;" and so are sin and its corruptions, the world and its temptations, the devil and his wiles, for us.

There are likewise some points of resemblance between God and this unjust judge. Long had he stood by and, without one effort on her behalf, seen this poor woman spurned and oppressed; and long also God seemed to stand by when his people were ground to the dust in Egypt; in old Pagan and in more modern Popish times, when their cruel enemies shed the blood of his saints like water, and, immured in dungeons, bleeding on scaffolds, hiding in the caves of our mountains, his elect cried to him day and night, and the Church, helpless as a widow, implored him, saying,

Avenge me of mine adversary! And this is true also of his dealings with individual believers. How long in their corruptions are the messengers of Satan left to buffet them? Weary of the struggle with some besetting sin, and hating it as a slave his cruel tyrant, they cry, "How long, O Lord, how long?" How often, all but despairing, are they ready to exclaim with Paul, "Who shall deliver me from the body of this death?"

But there are important points of disparity between this judge and our God: and in these I find assurance of final victory, and the highest encouragements to instant, constant, urgent, prayer. A bad man, with a heart cold as ice and hard as iron, was he moved by importunity to redress the wrongs of one for whom he felt no regard, whose happiness or misery was nothing to him?—how much more will God be importuned to grant our prayers! Just, and more than just, he is merciful and gracious, long-suffering and slow to wrath, abundant in goodness and in truth. He has no pleasure in the death of the wicked—he is willing that all should come to him and live—he waits to be gracious. Let his people trust in him, and wait on him. He may hide his face from them; it is but for a little. The dead, the widow's husband, never loved like the living God. Her wrongs did not disturb him in his grave; but ours move Jehovah in the heavens. Above the anthems of the celestial choir, he hears our feeblest cry; and amid the glories of the upper sanctuary, Christ's eye turns less on the glittering crowns his redeemed ones cast at his feet than on his people here—fighting in this field of battle, weeping in this vale of tears. Therefore let us pray on, nor cease praying till we cease living. He may address us as he did his mother, saying, Woman, my hour is not yet come; but come it shall. Rest assured that no prayer is lost; and let this help them that wait on the Lord to renew their strength, and in the hour of devotion to mount up with wings as eagles! If he spared not his own Son, shall he not with him also freely give us all things—and fulfill, at his own time and in his own way, these his own gracious words, "For the oppression of the poor and for the sighing of the needy, now will I arise, saith the Lord?"

When night fell on Jerusalem, and the tide and hum of business had ceased, and one after another the lights were extinguished, and all fires quenched in the sleeping city, one was kept alive—the fire that burned on God's holy altar. "It shall not be put out," said the Lord, "the fire shall ever be burning on the altar, it shall never go out." Fed by such logs as blazed on the hearths and roared in the chimneys of olden times, yet this had not been kindled by man's hands or blown into flame by his breath. Like God's love on a lost world, or his wrath on the head of his dying Son, it had descended from the skies. "There came," it is said, when Aaron and his sons were offering their first sacrifice, "fire out from before the Lord, and consumed the burnt-offering and the fat, which when the people saw, they shouted and fell on their face." Whether slumbering in its ashes or flaming with the fat of sacrifices, this fire burned by night and day on the altar; nor was it till after the lapse of nearly a thousand years that it went out—quenched, hissing in the blood of priests who fell in defence of the temple at the first captivity. Now in that old altar on which the sacred fire was always burning, but where sacrifices were not always offering, we see the heart of a devout believer. He is not always praying; but within his bosom there is a heaven-kindled love, fires of desire, fervent longings, which make him always ready to pray and often engage him in prayer. And thus he who engages in devout meditations and holds communion with God through his word and also through his works, may, in respect of his habitual, prevailing frame of mind, as well as of his frequent prayers, be said to "pray without ceasing," "always to pray;" he is like an Æolian harp, on whose strings, by night or day, the wind has but to breathe to wake up sweet and plaintive music.

In considering more particularly the lessons regarding prayer which our Lord told this parable to teach, I remark that

IT DOES NOT TEACH US TO PRAY.

There is no need it should; or that the Bible should —any more than it should prove, what it always assumes, the being of a God. Such a monster as an atheist, who denies that, it does not suppose to exist; nor any one, man or woman, who does not acknowledge, whether they practise it or not, the duty and necessity of prayer. Nor this without reason. Like the belief in a God, the moral sense of right and wrong, the hope of immortality, the expectation of a judgment, prayer seems as much an instinct of the soul as breathing, eating, drinking are instinctive actions of the body which we need neither to be told, nor to learn, to do. No doubt, men who would be "wise above what is written,"—prying into the secret things of God, and, like one who attempts to close his fingers on this big globe, attempting to grasp the infinite with finite minds, —have started objections to prayer. They ask, does God need to be told what we need? is man vain enough to suppose that his prayers can change the divine purposes? that creatures so feeble and insignificant as we can move the hand that moves the universe? or that our will can be of the smallest consequence to him who does everything according to the counsel and purpose of his own? It is not needful to answer such objections. I have read how a great poet, who was a sceptic, when he and Byron in a storm at sea expected every moment to be their last, dropt on his knees on 'the watery deck, and, beating his breast, cried passionately to God—the tempest blowing away, like cobwebs, his flimsy objections to prayer. In such hours Nature, rising in her might and majesty, asserts her supremacy; and the instinct of prayer bears a man over all these difficulties as on the crest of a mountain wave. With these, simple Christians give themselves no trouble; they are like an infant who knows nothing of the philosophy of sucking, nor waits to know it, but, so soon as put to a mother's breast, fastens on it. And it seems as natural for man to pray as for babes to suck —in his distress and danger to cry to God, as on falling into the water to make instinctive efforts to reach the rock for footing, or rise to the surface for breath.

Prayer belongs to a man as much as speech: for, as there was never a nation found, the rudest, most savage, in their habits and homes the nearest to the brutes, which did not speak; there never was a nation found, the rudest, most savage, in their homes and habits the least raised above the brutes, which did not pray.

IT TEACHES US HOW TO PRAY.

This subject, dividing itself like a tree into many branches, embraces the spring of prayer, which lies in our sense of need—the spirit of prayer, which consists in devout sincerity,—the object of prayer, which is our Father in heaven—the channel of prayer, which is his Son Jesus Christ, the mediator of the new Covenant. Important as these subjects are, this parable directs our attention to a matter belonging to prayer, not less important. The point here, is the fervor and frequency, the constancy and perseverance, or what has been called, in one word, the *importunity* of prayer. "He spake a parable unto them," says the Evangelist, "to this end, that men ought always to pray and not to faint"—to pray on, nor give up praying till they get the thing prayed for. This implies at least on our part,

STATED DAILY PRAYER.

It is in the morning and evening that Nature, who gives her nights to sleep and her days to work, pays, if I may so say, her worship to God. At dewy morn and eve, from their golden and silver censers, the flowers offer the incense of their fragrance, and skies and woods which were mute during the heat of the day and darkness of the night, break out into a melodious burst of song. The bird that, leaving God to care for it, sleeps with its head beneath its wing in the darkness, and spends the busy day gathering its food or catering for its young, drops at even from the skies, singing, into its grassy nest; and mounts thence at rosy dawn to praise God by the gate of heaven ere it begins the labors of the day. And so, in a way, does every man and woman who has the least pretension to a Christian's character—morning and evening find them on their knees before God. What day closes without many mercies to be grateful for, and many sins to be confessed and pardoned? and what day is entered on that has not burdens to be borne, and battles to be fought, to which it behoves us to go forth guided by the counsel, guarded by the power, strengthened by the grace, and defended, like a mail-clad warrior, from head to heel, by the whole armor of God? To omit prayer, is to go to battle having left our weapons behind us, in the tent; is to go to our daily labor without the strength imparted by a morning meal; is to attempt the bar where breakers roar and rocks hide their rugged heads without taking our pilot on board. If from a sense of weakness Moses, on Sinai's thundering, flashing, quaking, mount, exclaimed, "If thy presence go not with me, let us not go *up*," well may we say of the world, with its daily trials and temptations, works and warfare, Unless thy presence go with us, let us not go *down*. Therefore ought men, unless in very rare circumstances, always, morning and evening, to pray.

Thus, like soldiers on the morning of the conflict, we grind our swords for battle with the world, the devil, and the flesh; and thus, when the day's combat is over, retiring to pray, we apply a healing ointment, the balm of Gilead, to the wounds of conscience; and thus, as a begrimed workman on coming home repairs at even-tide to bathe in flowing river or swelling sea, we resort to prayer to wash away sin's daily, guilty stains in the fountain of Jesus' blood.

Judge Hale, one of the greatest ornaments of the English church and the English bench, in expressing the value he set on the Sabbath as a day, not of business or worldly recreation, but of holy rest, said that he found the work of the week go well according as the Sabbath had been kept well. For as I have seen one stroke of an eagle's wings send her, without further effort, sailing a long way on through the fields of air, the impulse which a well-spent sabbath gave him was sensibly felt throughout all the running week. As much may be said for daily prayers—the morning, elsewhere than in the skies, settling, for good or evil, for conquest or defeat, for progress or backsliding, the character of the coming day. Therefore ought men always to pray, morning and evening, day by day.

Are our bodies so constituted that the food of one day suffices for the wants of the next? Do even occasional banquets dispense with the necessity of daily bread? Are the arrangements of nature such that one bright day each week is enough—sufficient to melt the snows of winter, to turn the naked forests into a sea of foliage, or cover our fields in autumn with sheaves of golden corn? No; the body needs daily bread; fields for the ripening of their fruits, and gardens for the beauty of their flowers, need daily sunlight, if not sunshine. And the soul cannot thrive, nor its graces grow and ripen, without daily prayer to God and frequent communion with the skies. I say, therefore, we ought always to pray morning and evening at the least; so much oftener, so much the better—and the result, if it is devout, earnest, believing prayer, will be to maintain our spiritual life under what appears the most unfavorable circumstances. On the rocks by the sea-shore I have seen marine creatures living when the tide was out; not in the briny pools it leaves, but on the dry and naked rock—in the withering air—in the burning, broiling sun. They lived because, when twice each day the foaming tide came in, and rising, covered the rocky shelves they clung to, they opened their shut and shelly mouths to drink in water enough to last them when the tide went out, and till the next tide came in. Even so, twice a day also at the least, are we to replenish our thirsty souls,—fill our emptiness from the ocean of grace and mercy that flows, free and full in Christ, to the least of saints and chief of sinners. In Him dwelleth all the fullness of the Godhead bodily.

IT TEACHES PERSEVERING PRAYER.

What would be thought of a man who was ashamed to own his country, nor would take up even speech in her defence among strangers, in a foreign land? It is when broad seas part us from our native shores that the love of country burns strongest. Her songs sound sweetest in the exile's ear. Those faults of hers we lay bare at home, we conceal abroad; and, like dutiful sons, try to cast a mantle on her shame—hiding it from the eyes of aliens. We are not ashamed of our country; yet, alas! how many seem ashamed of their religion and their God? Some could hardly blush more to be caught stealing than they would do to be caught praying—starting from their knees like men engaged in some guilty thing. And how many young men and women, abandoning the praying habits of their early life and a pious home, have been lost through this false and coward shame? Insult their country, they will resent the offence—the poorest Highlander standing up for the honor of clan and chief, nor consenting, without a bleeding heart, to be torn from the barren and stormy rocks to which his affections cling. Would God our piety were as fervent and brave as our patriotism! But, thrown into the company of strangers, perhaps of the ungodly, shrinking lest these should wonder at them or make them butts for ridicule, some steal to bed and leave it without bending the knees in prayer. This is to repeat the crime of Peter, and say, amid scenes where Christ is insulted by his enemies and should be boldly honored by his friends, I know not the man.

If it is right for men, as an old heathen says, to learn from an enemy, it is right for Christians to learn from such as are ignorant of their faith, or hostile to it. And how might it bring a blush to a coward's cheek to see the poor Mahometan—in company as in solitude, on the mart of commerce or on the muddy street, on the slippery deck or on the sandy desert, wherever he is and before whomsoever he is, beggar or king, pagan or Christian—drop on his knees at sundown to offer his devotions, ready rather to die than miss them; like a wise man, counting them, not his shame, but glory. If, boasting of their villanies, of their feats of dissipation and debauchery, of their triumphs over simple innocence, unsuspecting virtue, the flowers they have vilely plucked to cast on the streets when their bloom was gone, bad men glory in their shame, shall Christians be ashamed of their glory? God forbid! Show the world your colors—fling out the blood-dyed, time-honored banner, saying—

> "I'm not ashamed to own my Lord,
> Or to defend his cause,
> Maintain the glory of his cross,
> And honor all his laws."

As to the point especially in hand—persevering prayer—the very heathens seem, more than many professing Christians, to appreciate its power and value. A traveller, for instance, who was lately exploring some of the loftiest valleys of the Himalayas, found a tribe close by the regions of eternal snow, whose religion had a feature that struck him with great surprise. Indeed, he sneers at it; though no man's faith should be turned to ridicule, or even lightly assailed, unless care is taken to substitute something better in its place. It may be a false hope; yet it is his all. It may be a dream; yet it is a happy one—soothing the sorrows of life, and scattering some beautiful, though fading flowers along the margin of its rugged path. Then what is the crime of those who in these days recklessly cast doubts on the Christian faith, and start difficulties in the minds of simple, unlearned ones, which I can answer, but they cannot? How cruel to disturb their peace who were quietly, and usefully, and hopefully, and happily, holding on their course to heaven? It is no light thing to shake a man's confidence in what he believes to be the Word of God—in a book which he clasps to his bosom as life's greatest treasure, and will lay below his head as death's softest pillow. It requires no great ability to do this wrong. The puniest buzzing insect may annoy us by its tiny sting; and many a man's peace may be disturbed by objections by which, thank God, it cannot be destroyed.

What excited both the surprise and sneers of the traveller in the religion of these Indian mountains, was the practice the people followed of praying by machinery. Certain prayers were placed on revolving cylinders; and as the wheel went round, and the prayer came up, each time its face turned to heaven, God was supposed to read it. It was as good as spoken by living lips. While engaged in his work, or passing the cylinder at intervals, the worshiper from time to time gave it a turn so as to keep it almost constantly spinning on its axis. Others more devout and still more ingenious, improving on that, set the cylinder in the run of a stream, that, as it turned like a mill-wheel, prayer might be offered day and night continually. Well, though it may be a bold thing to say, I would rather, in that rude way, "pray without ceasing," than like some, never pray at all—in other words, I would rather live and die a devout pagan than an undevout Christian. No doubt the mind of the Indian who trusts to such prayers may be dark as his tawny skin; and, not proceeding from the heart, they may leave it cold as the snows, and hard as the rocks among which, remote from the Christian world, he holds his mountain fastness. But, not to say that the prayers of our lips may be as formal and lifeless as those of the Buddhist's wheel, rude as is the method of his worship, and dark as may be the mind of the worshiper, there is a glimmering here of these truths—"instant in prayer," "pray without ceasing"—"men ought always to pray, and not to faint."

It is hard, fainting work, praying. It is harder work to pray than preach; since for one who could pray well, I will get you a hundred who could preach well a whole hour. How much easier for the sailor to watch the night through on the rolling deck, the sentinel on the beleaguered wall, than, with John Welsh in Ayr's old church, alone, in the darkness, with the town sleeping in their houses, and the dead around sleeping in their graves, to pass a whole night on our knees?

We ask, and receive not. Why? Because, says the Apostle, we ask amiss. We do not believe what we profess; nor feel what we say; nor wish what we ask —or, if we do, we do not take the right way of getting it. And how can we expect God to answer prayer when he sees, what we ourselves might see, that we are not earnest? If we were, we would be urgent—praying in the house, by the way, on our beds, at our business—prayer, sounding or silent, a constant flowing stream. By constant dropping, the water wears a hole in the hardest stone. By constant growing, the tree-root rends the hardest rocks asunder. And who, as he sat on a jutting crag amid the spray of the roaring, flashing cataract, has not marked how by her constant flow the river has polished its rugged sides, and worn out smooth runnels for its streams? With such a feeble power, through the force of continued action, how great the results? That rock, indeed, is no more a symbol of the kind heart of God than this unjust judge is, in character, a type of Him who is, I repeat it, not unjust, but just; nor merely just, but merciful and gracious, long-suffering, and slow to wrath, abundant in goodness and in truth. Yet, as it is only perseverance in grace that can carry us up to heaven, it is only perseverance in prayer that can bring its blessings down. Such is the plan of redemption, the ordinance of God—"The kingdom of heaven suffereth violence, and the violent take it by force."

VI.

The Parable of the Pharisee and the Publican.

Luke xviii. 9-14.

NATURE divides our globe into different belts of vegetation. Each zone has plants peculiar to itself. Under and beside the burning line lies the region of palms and bananas; then appear the vine and olive; then the oak and chestnut; the forests of evergreen of pine, with fields of hardy oats; then the birch with its silver dress and the mountain-ash with its coral berries, dwarfing away as you approach the pole—till they vanish; and, the utmost limits of vegetation reached, you enter the domain of eternal winter, snow and ice, silence and death. While there is only one bird that, a citizen of the world, frequents every shore, there is not one plant, so far as I know, that inhabits every country. Plants grow only in certain soils, or at certain heights, or under certain lines of latitude. Unlike these, pride is a weed that, springing up in every heart, grows at all elevations—as well in the humblest as in the highest stations of life; and under every system of religion, the true as well as the false. Strange to say, it is often found where it seems to have nothing to feed on, where there is the least occasion and the least excuse for it—like the wallflower rooted in the crevices of shattered rock or mouldering tower, it seems to grow best on ruins. Never till man fell, did he form the ambitious project of building a tower whose top should reach to heaven.

Pride is a sin of the heart; and while in his prayer, "Cleanse thou me from secret errors, keep back thy servant also from presumptuous sins," David showed himself alive to the dangers of such sins, others, in guarding only against the temptation to gross offences, leave themselves exposed to what is their greatest danger. Lodged in the heart like a robber who has concealed himself in some dark recess, and waits till nightfall to seize the plunder, this sin is more likely than many others to escape our notice. Not entailing the loss of character, or health, or wealth, which are the common penalties of crime, it can be indulged in with apparent impunity. Not always early or easily detected, this vice sometimes indeed assumes the features of a virtue—apes a noble independence of spirit, self-respect, a due regard to our rank and position; nay, even a sacred respect to God's truth, to purity of doctrine or holiness of life. In Herod it wore the mask of conscience, and for his oath's sake he beheaded John; in the Jews, of a tender regard for God's honor, and they would have no dealings with the Samaritans; in the Pharisee, of purity of life, and so, sailing magnificently past the woman that was a sinner, lest his robes should be defiled by the touch of hers, he warns her off, saying, Stand aside, I am holier than thou. Obtaining access to hearts which would close the door in the face of grosser vices, pride, besides, is a very dreadful and deadly sin. Has it not proved itself so? It cost Nebuchadnezzar his reason; in his successors it cost Hezekiah his kingdom; on Galilee it nearly cost Simon Peter his life; taking root in the hearts of our first parents, it cost them and mankind Eden; springing up in angels' bosoms, it cost them heaven. And as the wary mariner, dreading it more than lowering skies or stormy sea, takes alarm at the first sign of the leak which, hid beneath the surface and gaping by the keel, admits the water into the hold, our Lord, alarmed, if I may say so, at the first signs of this insidious and fatal sin in his disciples, promptly proceeds to stop the evil; and for this purpose, to instruct, warn, and alarm them, he relates the parable of the Pharisee and the Publican.

Before studying these two characters in their order, let us take a general survey of the religion of the Pharisees, and attend to such practical lessons as it is calculated to suggest and teach.

THEIR RELIGION HAD NOT ITS SEAT IN THE HEART.

Baron Humboldt mentions a remarkable custom of some of the native tribes of America—one that would have carried our thoughts homeward as much as a daisy springing from the sod of their prairies, or a lark singing in Indian skies. Some time after a child is born, a font full of water is brought into the tent, and a fire kindled on its floor. The babe is then taken from its mother's arms, not to be burned or drowned, but plunged over head into the water and swung rapidly through the flames. In this custom, which is practised on all their children, we see a rude baptismal rite: nor is it possible to read of it and still less were it possible to see this ceremony without recalling the words of John: "He shall baptize you with the Holy Ghost and with *fire;*" and those of Christ Himself: "Except a man be born of *water* and of the Spirit, he cannot enter into the kingdom of God." As I have seen an insect that may have fluttered among the flowers of Eden, or perished amidst the waters of the flood, embalmed in amber, in this custom we seem to see, embalmed in tradition, a fragment of patriarchal piety, and of the divine truths which man knew when the ancestors of these Indians—perhaps the world's earliest emigrants— left the cradle of mankind. It is a symbolical confession of human depravity, and of the necessity that the soul should be purified as by fire and water from inborn corruption; and to witness this remarkable rite among these distant heathen could hardly fail to transport us on the wings of fancy to the old church at home, where a father was holding up his babe for baptism, or the voices of the great congregation were singing to some familiar, plaintive tune,

> Behold I in iniquity
> Was formed the womb within,
> My mother also me conceived
> In guiltiness and sin.

How strange to turn to the Pharisees, and find them, with the Word of God in their hands, apparently more ignorant than those painted savages—illustrating the paradox of Scripture: "They have eyes but they see not, ears but they hear not, and minds but they do not understand." They were profoundly ignorant of the plague of their own hearts. They did not feel the need of being renewed, or know that religion cannot live anywhere but in the heart, and lies in nothing so much as a heart right with God. Even Nicodemus seemed ignorant of this. When informed by our Lord that he must be born again, he was surprised, filled with astonishment; and with a simplicity which we might expect, and would excuse in a child, replied, "How can a man be born when he is old? Can he enter a second time into his mother's womb and be born?" If it was thus with him—a ruler in Israel, a man who felt such an interest in religion that he sought our Lord, though under the cloak of night, what must it have been with others? How appropriate to the followers of such leaders, the question, "If the light that is in you be darkness, how great is that darkness!"

It was great, gross, darkness. The religion of these Pharisees consisting of mere ceremonial observances, lying in such matters as meats and drinks, washing platters, paying tithes and keeping fasts, the worst passions were left to rage and burn within their hearts—as do volcanic fires beneath the purple vineyards and green forests of Vesuvius' slopes. Outwardly saints, they were inwardly devils. And lest I should be considered uncharitable, let us hear his account of them, who in the fullness of his tenderness and mercy promised Paradise to a dying thief, and turned eyes of pity on the woman that was a sinner. "Woe unto you, Scribes and Pharisees, hypocrites," said our Lord, "for ye are like unto whited sepulchres, which indeed appear beautiful outward, but within are full of dead men's bones and of all uncleanness. Even so ye also appear outwardly righteous unto men, but within ye are full of hypocrisy and iniquity. Fill ye up the measure of your fathers. Ye serpents, ye generation of vipers, how can ye escape the damnation of hell."

THEIR RELIGION LAY IN OUTWARD ACTS OF WORSHIP AND A SCRUPULOUS OBSERVANCE OF ITS FORMS.

In one of our late Indian battles, a native officer lay mortally wounded on the field beside one of our own. Exhausted with loss of blood and exposed to the fierce rays of a burning sun, both were tortured with thirst. One, whose motions they eagerly watched, at length approached them with a supply of water. After our countryman had taken a long, deep draught, it was presented to the Hindoo. He had been crying for water, and had it now. Yet, ere he drinks, he turns a dying eye on the Good Samaritan to ask his caste. It is low; and his religion forbids him to take meat or drink from such impure hands. Our countryman, seeing him hesitate, remonstrates—telling how it will assuage his sufferings, and may save his life: but remonstrates in vain. The other turns one greedy look on the blessed water, and pours it out on the ground—a sacrifice to the claims of conscience. And esteeming a devout Pagan a better man in God's sight than a careless, unconscientious Christian, I say, whatever judgment others may pronounce on this act, would God that Christ's followers were as ready to take up their cross, deny themselves daily, and follow Jesus; dying with Him rather than denying Him!

The scrupulous observance which the Pharisees paid to mere forms, has no such claims on our respect. They knew, or ought to have known, better. Yet, neglecting the moral law and even violating its plainest precepts, they made religion lie wholly in ritual observances and certain outward acts of worship. They gave alms. They prayed often. They fasted and paid tithes; fasting oftener and paying tithes on more things than even the law required—as if they would make God their debtor. They were scrupulously careful to avoid any ceremonial uncleanness; and that was one reason perhaps why the priest and Levite left the wounded man on the road, lest the touch of what might be a dead body should render them unclean. They were particularly careful also to observe all ceremonial duties; and therefore the murderers of our Lord, with his blood still red on their guilty hands, sought to have his body removed from the cross, and respect rendered to the law which required that whosoever was hanged should be taken down by sunset. They were close attenders also on the temple, where, as in a Roman Catholic church, with a crowd of worshipers, on their knees, telling their beads, repeating their prayers with eyes cast on the ground or raised to an image, there was great appearance of devotion. Apparently abstracted from all sublunary things, with hands and eyes raised to heaven, with loud and sonorous voice sounding forth his prayer, with texts of Scripture sown on his dress, and ashes sprinkled on his head, there stood the Pharisee—a living lie—a whited sepulchre, with a head as dark and a heart as foul as the grave.

Lights are kindled on the seaboard, some to guide the ship in, others to warn her off: this burns at the harbor's mouth, and that, a beacon of danger, flashes where the sea breaks foaming on a fatal reef. And the Pharisees have left us, not an example to follow, but to avoid. How does their case warn the churches against attaching much importance to religious forms, either in the way of unreasonably adhering to such as are old, or unnecessarily introducing such as are new. It is in the nature of a religion of many forms to degenerate into one of form. By occupying and indeed engrossing the attention of the worshiper, they withdraw it from the state of his heart, and prove as pernicious to true piety as a superabundance of leaves to the plant, whose sap is spent on feeding the leaf, to the detriment of the fruit: and perhaps some churches might be benefited by a free use of the knife with which the gardener prunes away the flush of green wood to increase the crop of fruit. I see much danger in a multiplicity, but little, or none, in a variety of forms. Unity with variety is God's law in the kingdom of nature; and why should not his law in the kingdom of grace be unity of spirit with variety of forms? Uniformity is but the shadow of unity: and how often have churches in vain attempts after the first, lost the second—like the dog in the fable lost both? At the Lord's table I have knelt with Episcopalians, I have sat with Presbyterians, and I have stood with fellow-worshipers in a foreign church under the shadow of the Alps; and I can only pity the person who, believing in the communion of the saints, could find in the attitude any reason for not engaging in the ordinance. This were to be great in little things; and forget that Christian love and charity which are the weightier matters of the law. It may be that the forms of worship in some of our churches are, as is alleged, bald and bare. If so, there is no reason why this should not be amended. But there is much reason why we should beware, on the one hand, of putting uniformity of worship in room of the unity of the spirit, and, on the other, of substituting dead forms for a living faith. Let us never forget that forms are not religion, but only its drapery; and that, as they dress children lightly who wish to brace their frames, as the laborer throws off his coat to work, and as in the ancient games the candidates stepped into the race-course unencumbered with many, or heavy, garments, the fewer forms which religion wears, consistent with decency and order, the more robust she will grow—she will work with greater energy—and, like one of beautiful mould and symmetry, she will walk with more native, queenly, grace —when

Unadorned, adorned the most.

THEIR RELIGION WAS CHARACTERIZED BY OSTENTATION.

The Pharisees distributed charity; but it was to the sound of a trumpet, seeking the praise of men under pretence of caring for the poor;—therefore our Lord said, "When thou doest thine alms, do not sound a trumpet before thee, as the hypocrites do in the synagogues, and in the streets, that they may have glory of men." They fasted; but not from sin;—therefore our Lord, detecting "the lust of the eyes and the pride of life" looking out from the holes of their rueful mask, warned his disciples, saying: "When ye fast be not as the hypocrites, of a sad countenance, for they disfigure their faces that they may appear unto men to fast." They prayed; not that they might be pardoned of God, but praised of men, and gaining a character for piety, gain the widow's esteem for the villanous purpose of plundering her house. Their humility was but the stepping-stone of their ambition—tigers, they crouched to make the surer, deadlier, spring; and therefore our Lord warned his disciples, saying, "Thou shalt not be as the hypocrites, for they love to pray standing in the synagogues and in the corners of the street, that they may be seen of men." That they may be seen of men! he rings the changes on that—exposing the pride and vanity that lay at the root of their religion. Loud, ostentatious, and unprofitable, it was like the brawling, noisy, foaming, frothy torrent, which, with a rock for its bed and barrenness on its banks, makes itself seen and heard. How different genuine, gracious piety! Affluent in blessings but retiring from observation, it has its symbol in the stream that pursues a silent course, and, flashing out in the light of day but here and there, but now and then, is not known but by the good it does—the flowers that bloom on its banks, and the evergreen verdure which it gives to the pastures through which it winds on its quiet path.

To appreciate the justice of these remarks, we have only to look at the sect in the specimen of it this parable presents. Judging the stock by the sample, look at

THE PHARISEE.

Sweeping contemptuously by others who, feeling themselves unworthy to tread the holy courts, worshiped reverently at a distance, he makes his way to the front, pride in his eye, and self-complacency in his bearing; and now beyond the vulgar throng, he stands to begin his devotions, not only to pray thus *with* himself, but that he might be the observed of all observers *by* himself—an interpretation of the words which betrays no lack of charity, since our Lord has told us that the Pharisees did pray to be seen of men. There is often a great incongruity between the language of our prayers and the state of our hearts— the one, alas, is so much more devout than the other. But there was no inconsistency here. Out of the abundance of the heart the mouth spake here; and seldom has God listened to such an offensive outpouring of pride and arrogance. Observe *first* the fashion and form of his prayer. In a sense, it is no prayer—it contains neither confession nor petition; there is neither guilt acknowledged nor pardon asked; it expresses no want, and it asks no help. No doubt there is an acknowledgment of divine goodness—God is mentioned, is thanked; yet there is no redeeming point in this. Under a flimsy pretense of glorifying God, he glorifies himself, and as to his expression of thanks, I regard that as on a par with those professions of humility in which many vain men are in the habit of indulging; and which are but a cover, and a very transparent one, for their self-conceit—for telling what feeds their vanity and is intended to exalt themselves. To thank God is right. We have much to thank him for; and had the Pharisee said, God, I thank thee that I am not in hell, that thou hast not dealt with me according to my sins, that thou hast so restrained the corruptions of this wicked heart as to keep me back from presumptuous, flagrant sins—if the thought of others had excited such gratitude in his heart as was expressed by one who, seeing a felon led to the gallows, exclaimed, speaking of himself, But for the grace of God, there goes John Bradford!—imperfect as his prayer was, on that one leg it might have limped to heaven. Done in the spirit that does not despise but pity the wicked, to thank God that we are not as they are is a pious thing. All are hewn out of the same rock, and dug out of the hole of the same pit; and the purest woman therefore has cause to thank God that she is not as the basest of her sex; nor is there a good man who has been preserved from becoming, like some of his early associates, a wreck of character, of body, of soul, but, as he sees in their fate what his might have been, will thank God that he is not as others—giving the glory where it is due; saying, with the apostle, "By grace I am what I am."

Secondly, observe the substance of his prayer. He tells God how he fasted and paid tithes. And if religion lay in abstaining from food but not from sin, in giving our property but not our hearts to God, he was indeed a religious man—and more religious than may at first appear. The Mosaic economy, which is misrepresented by many as a system of great austerity, established numerous feasts during which the people, set loose from toil and arrayed in holiday attire, were to eat of the fat and drink of the sweet and pass their time in innocent pleasures. It enjoined but one fast —only one in the whole fifty-two weeks of the year. But this Pharisee, not content with fasting once each year as the law required, fasted twice each week; and, teaching us to set little value on such ritual observances, the fasts that starved his body seem only to have fed his pride; the austerities which mortified his flesh became the means of gratifying his vanity. He showed a corresponding excess of zeal in the matter of tithes. God required his people to tithe the fruits of the olive and vine, the sheaves of the field and the produce of their flocks: but as in those countries where, devoted to a life of celibacy, men immure themselves in monasteries, and women wither in convents, the sacrifices of the Pharisee rose above the requirements of the law—anise and cummin and other common pot-herbs were all scrupulously tithed. Hence his boast, I fast *twice* a week, and pay tithes of *all* that I possess. In other words: What a good man I am; let others acknowledge their shortcomings; as for me, I dread not a day of count and reckoning; for me, the day of judgment that brings man face to face with God has no terrors; I have done more than he requires; He is my debtor rather than I his—the balance will stand in my favor. What great, swelling words of vanity! How may we apply to this miserable self-deceiver, and to all that self-righteous class of whom, though the pride of their hearts may not be so fully developed, he is the type, our Lord's language to the Laodiceans, "Thou sayest, I am rich, and increased with goods, and have need of nothing: and knowest not that thou art wretched, and miserable, and poor, and blind, and naked." So we might dismiss him to make way for a better man—praying God by his Holy Spirit to keep us not only from the lust of the flesh and the lust of the eye, but also from the pride of life.

But we are not done with the Pharisee. He has certain negative as well as positive merits. Here is what he is not, "I am not as other men are." To entertain a bad opinion of others without sufficient evidence proves more than the lack of the charity which hopeth all things, and believeth all things. Who does not believe others virtuous would be found, were the secrets of his heart and life known, to be himself vicious. We may lay it down as an axiom, that those who are ready to suspect others of being actuated by a regard to self-interest, are themselves selfish. Thieves do not believe in the existence of honesty; nor rakes in virtue; nor mercenary politicians in patriotism; and the reason why worldlings regard religious people as hypocrites is their own want of religion—knowing that were they to profess a warm regard for Christ, the glory of God, and the salvation of souls, they would be hypocrites, they conclude others to be so. Hence also you find many novelists representing every man into whose mouth they put the language of piety as either a rogue or a fool, most commonly a rogue—a very unsound but not unnatural conclusion on their part; for prejudices resemble the fogs that turn the bright sun into a dull, copper ball, and a bad heart is like the jaundice that sees its own dingy yellow in the purest lily. I conclude, therefore, however fair the whited sepulchre looked, that in his heart at least this Pharisee was, what he took other men to be—an extortioner, unjust, and an adulterer. He had no right to put on such airs, or, as his eye fell on him, to make a footstool of the publican to stand higher before God—saying by way of climax, "nor as this publican."

In this proud, arrogant man we see the spirit of self-righteousness fully developed. Although they may not come out so prominently, the elements of his character are in all who trust in themselves for salvation. May God enlighten our eyes, show us ourselves! For who knows himself, knowing much more ill of himself than he can of any one else, will indulge in no such proud, and self-complacent and odious comparisons—his prayer will be that of David, Enter not into judgment with thy servant, for in thy sight shall no man living be justified—his language that of Job, I abhor myself—his confession, Ezra's, O my God, I am ashamed, and blush to lift up my face to thee, my God—and glad to enter heaven at the back of Manasseh, or the woman that was a sinner, or the thief of the cross, he will leave the Pharisee to place himself beside the publican, and catch from his lips the heartfelt prayer, God be merciful to me a sinner!

THE PUBLICAN.

The white trimmings on a coffin catch the eye; and pure as it seems when, falling softly, it lies level on the fields, or the sport of wintry winds, has been tossed into fantastic wreaths, snow never looks so white as in the church-yard—beside the black mould and gaping mouth of a new-dug grave. Studying effect, the painter and orator make use of such strong contrasts: and no doubt it was for this purpose that the Pharisee dragged the publican into his prayer, using him as a foil to set off himself—a dark and sombre background to present his merits in a more striking light. In this, "He made a pit and digged it, and is fallen into the ditch which he made." The Pharisee becomes a background to set off the publican; and never did humility appear more beautiful in the eyes of God and man than here, where it stands contrasted with the empty vanity and haughty arrogance of this inflated Pharisee. In illustration of this, observe

THE MANNER OF HIS PRAYER.

He stood afar off.—Both prayed standing, teaching us that that attitude, which was the one commonly assumed by the Jews in the temple, is one which we may use with propriety in public worship. It is equally with kneeling an attitude of worship—though the latter may be more suitable for prayer where the congregation stand up to sing. There is propriety, but there can be no devotion in an attitude. Man looketh on the outward appearance, but God looketh on the heart; and the only rule applicable to such matters as are not the weighty matters of the law, is to assume the attitude which rather aids than hinders devotion, and avoid that, which, acting through the senses, disturbs the mind. That posture is the best which least distracts attention by a feeling of bodily weariness, or otherwise drags our thoughts downward—hanging like a dead weight on the wings of prayer.

But while both stood, the publican stood *afar off*, as one who felt himself unworthy to enter the house of God—as a beggar with the mud of the road on his shoes and the rags of poverty on his back might hang about the door of a lordly hall, and, oppressed with a sense of his meanness, modestly decline the invitation to enter. Men often, very often, speak more eloquently by acts than words; and in the arrestment of his steps, in the reverential distance at which he stands, the poor publican seems to say, I am less than the least of all thy mercies. Blessed are the poor in spirit! It is to him and all such as come modestly in to seat themselves down, if I may say so, at the lower end of the table, that the Lord, who has his eye on them, will send the message, " Come ye up hither!"—for, while every one that exalteth himself shall be abased, he that humbleth himself shall be exalted.

He would not lift up so much as his eyes to heaven. —The Pharisee looked boldly up. Why not? There was nothing in heaven's cloudless azure purer than himself. No doubt the angels veil their faces with their wings; but there is no brightness in God's glory, sunlike, to dazzle him—nor awfulness in God's holiness to daunt him. Standing to God in the relation of a creditor rather than a debtor, why should he be ashamed to look him in the face? Fasting twice a week, and paying tithes of all that he possessed, he has not overdrawn but overpaid his accounts—doing more than the law required. Turn now to the publican, and what a contrast! There, like one caught in some act which overwhelms with a sense of shame, and covers the cheek with burning blushes, he stands with his head bent and his eyes cast on the ground. Self-accused, self-abased, and self-condemned, he shrinks within himself, and wonders perhaps that the very earth does not open its mouth to swallow him up. He does not dare to look up. But though his eyes are not lifted to heaven, his heart is; and, while he seems ready to sink to the ground, his soul is soaring aloft on the wings of prayer, upward to the heaven of heavens.

He smote upon his breast.—The hands of the Pharisee are stretched to heaven to receive the reward he expects at God's. There he stands, proud as the victor who, covered with the blood of a hundred battles and the laurels of a hundred victories, only bends his head to receive the crown from a king whose throne and whose country his valor has defended; and from whose hands he accepts the proudest honor, not so much as a matter of grace as of right. The hands of the publican are otherwise employed—he smote upon his breast. By this action, or by smiting on the thigh, the impassioned natives of the East expressed the deepest sorrow. But these sounding blows expressed more than sorrow. They said, as they fell thick and heavy on his bosom, Here lies the root of all my sins —O, this hard, foul, wicked heart!—My life has been bad, but it has been worse—here lies the inner spring of all these polluted streams! These blows were inarticulate prayers. They sounded forth to God's ear such wishes as these: "Create in me a clean heart and renew a right spirit within me." It had surely been done; for it was from the bosom which he smote that there went up to heaven, like an arrow from the bow-string, this brief, but blessed believing prayer:

GOD BE MERCIFUL TO ME A SINNER.

Earnestness does not express itself in long, inflated, pompous sentences. It is brief; it is simple. The moment has arrived when victory, long doubtful as the tide of success ebbed and flowed, may be won by one splendid, dashing, daring attack—the order is given in one brief word, Charge! On the distant waves a flag is seen now sinking in the trough and again rising on the crest of the foaming billows; and beneath that signal, clinging to the fragment of a vessel that lies many fathoms down in the depths of ocean, are two human forms—and all the cry that sounds from stem to stern is, A wreck, a wreck! and all the order, Lower the boat!—words hardly uttered when she drops on the water, and, pulled by stout rowers, is leaping over the waves to the rescue. One late in the deserted streets sees the smoke creep, and the flames begin to flash and flicker from a house whose tenants are buried in sleep; he bounds to the door and thunders on it—all his cry, Fire, Fire! Peter sinks amid the boisterous waves of Galilee and all the prayer of lips the cold water kisses is, as he stretches out his hand to Jesus, Save me, I perish! And with the brief, urgent, earnestness of one who seeing his danger, knows that there is no time, and believing in God's great mercy, feels that there is no need for long prayers, the publican, like a man who in falling over a crag catches the arm of a friendly tree, throws his whole soul into this cry, these few, blessed, accepted words, "God be merciful to me, a sinner!"

Both have prayed, and our Lord tells us the result. Insulting to God and man, the prayer of the Pharisee, like a stone cast at heaven, falls back and returns to break his own head—while the Publican's ascends like the cloud of incense that floated away fragrant and heavenward from the morning or evening sacrifice. Perfumed with a Saviour's merits, it is accepted as a sweet-smelling savor, and sins confessed are sins forgiven. Not that his confession and sorrow were the price of pardon; but that, feeling undone and lost, he cast himself on divine mercy, and so became a partaker of the righteousness which Jesus Christ has provided for the chief of sinners.

Thus he went down to his house "justified;" and so may we all—with a pardon in our bosoms and the peace of God in our hearts. Ah, that were the happiest home-going we ever made—sufficient to turn the barest hovel into a palace, and impart to the humblest fare more enjoyment than sumptuous banquets afford. Light is the step of one before whom the prison gates roll open, leaving him to walk forth to life and liberty. The sun never shone so bright, the flowers by the wayside never looked so beautiful, the birds in sky and merry woodland never sang so sweet, nor did love to everything ever glow and burn so in his bosom, as now, when taking an everlasting leave of strong jail and gloomy cell, he hastens home to embrace his wife and little ones—goes down to his house a free, pardoned, happy, blessed, man. Yet lighter his steps, and happier his heart, who, accepting Christ in God's house, goes down justified to his own. And what should hinder us? We have only to throw away all confidence in ourselves; and with confidence throw ourselves at Jesus's feet, or rather into his open arms, on his loving bosom—on which, when the work of our sanctification is completed, we shall be borne up to another and a better house, there to be crowned with everlasting glory and dwell forever with the Lord. Thus, while casting the proud down into hell God abases them, he will exalt the humble—them, and them only.

He dwelleth with such as are of an humble and contrite spirit; and they only with whom he dwells on earth, shall dwell with him in heaven.

I cannot close these observations without remarking that the Pharisees, of whom the man before us is a specimen, have furnished the world with a term wherewith to reproach those whose religion is less loose than its own. Such as are for living a strict and pure and holy life, who, believing that no man on his death-bed ever found that he had given too much time to God and Christ, the interest of his soul, and that eternal world on whose verge he stands, wish the Sabbath day to be spent in the public or private exercises of God's worship, such as seek to remove all temptations to spend it otherwise—whether in the form of theatres, or museums, public-gardens or public-houses, such men are opprobriously called Pharisees. Now, not to say that it is a bad cause which needs to be supported by calling bad names, this application of the term betrays, as I undertake and proceed to show, the grossest ignorance.

The Pharisees cared nothing for the poor. Does this character apply most to those who are called Pharisees, or to those who call them so? Which of these two classes are most frequently found imparting both material and spiritual comforts to the desolate abodes of poverty, I would leave the poor to say. It is no breach of charity to fancy them turning from those called Pharisees to such as call them so, to say, "Jesus we know, and Paul we know—these others we know—but who are ye?"

Again, the Pharisees, devouring widows' houses, made religion a mere pretense to promote their own secular and selfish ends. Now let impartial history say, whether in the dark days of trial, in times that demanded a noble self-denial, those called Pharisees, or those calling them so, have been the most ready to sacrifice their interests to their religion, their place to their principles, and leave father and mother, wife and children, houses and lands, to take up their cross and follow Christ.

Again, the Pharisees were sensual and self-indulgent. "They bound," said our Lord, "heavy burdens, and laid them on men's shoulders, but they themselves would not move them with one of their fingers." And do those whom the world calls Pharisees ask others to make efforts on behalf of humanity or of religion, while they themselves make none? Are theirs the names you miss in the lists of public charities? Do they bear the least part of such burdens? I venture to affirm the contrary: and that, were their support withdrawn, many of our philanthropic and religious schemes would tumble into ruins, like an arch deprived of its piers.

Again, the Pharisees were men of low *morale*; and therefore our Lord said, "Except your righteousness exceed the righteousness of the Scribes and Pharisees, ye shall in no wise enter into the kingdom of heaven." Now are those whom the world reproaches as such, less moral than those who reproach them? As a class, do their greater sins distinguish them from others as much as their greater professions? In the upper ranks of society, are impurity and loose morals more characteristic of those who keep the Lord's day sacred, than of those who make it one of business or of pleasure? and among the lower classes, is it those who resort to the church or to the public house on the Sabbath, who supply most work to the police and the greatest number of tenants to the prison?

Again, the Pharisees persecuted piety, and hating Jesus because he was holier than they, called him bad names, imputed to him bad motives, and held him up to public scorn—charging him with crimes which his soul abhorred, and of which he was innocent as the babe unborn. Now are those whom the world calls Pharisees, haters of serious and pure religion? Is it their pens and tongues which are dipped in poison, and employed to wound Christ in his members? Are they the successors of the men who, hating religion in their hearts and feeling that Christ's holy and unselfish life condemned theirs, crowned his forehead with thorns, and cried, Away with him to the cross?

Again, the Pharisees were a self-righteous class. They trusted to their own works for salvation, and were, however little occasion they had to be so, remarkably well pleased with themselves. Puffed up with vanity, they thanked God that they were not as others who might need a Saviour—they did not. But whoever found these to be the features of such as the world calls Pharisees? On the contrary, is not Jesus Christ and him crucified the very centre of their religion—the sun of their sky—the foundation of their most precious hopes? Disclaiming all self-confidence and merit in their own works, may not their creed be summed up in the words of him who raised himself on his dying bed to exclaim with life's latest breath, None but Christ, none but Christ! Let the world call white black, or light darkness, or sweet bitter, but not such men Pharisees. The north and south poles are not farther asunder.

Inapplicable as is such an epithet to devout Christians, let them beware how they furnish any, the least occasion for others using it by any inconsistency between their profession and their practice—by magnifying little things and overlooking the weightier matters of the law—by straining at a gnat, and swallowing a camel. Never overlook the difference between what is vital in divine truth and what is indifferent in human forms. Never mistake the dead robes for the living body of religion. Never forget that "to do justly and love mercy and walk humbly before God," is what the Lord requires of thee; that faith without works is dead; that form without spirit is dead; and that, the highest piety being ever associated with the deepest humility, true religion is like that sweetest of all singing-birds, the skylark, which with the lowest nest but highest wing dwells on the ground, and yet soars to the skies.

VII.

The Parable of the Hid Treasure.

Matthew xiii. 44.

ONE of the most beautiful legends of old times is that of the Golden Age. As sung by the heathen poets, this once was a happy world; its earliest periods being like the bright dawn of a dark and cloudy day; cheerful and happy, as the infancy of a life which afterwards grows beset with troubles and stained by crime. In these days, envy and strife and war were unknown; the habits of men were simple, their wants were few, their lives were virtuous: no slaves toiled in chains, nor captives pined in dungeons, nor bloody tyrants reigned on thrones; plenty filled every cup to the brim, and peace, unbroken by the strife of tongues or clash of arms, brooded on every shore. In contrast with those which followed them and went by the name of the Iron, these happy times were called the Golden Age. No poet's dream, this, like many other legends preserved in ancient song, is a fragment of true history, and one in which it is not difficult to recognize a tradition of Eden, and of man's early innocence—changed, no doubt, from its original form, as like a stone in the bed of a river, it has come rolling down the long and turbulent stream of time.

Literally, as well as figuratively, the earliest periods of the world were the Golden Age : for the discoveries of archæologists show that man's acquaintance with the metals began with gold and silver. Long ere he had forged iron into sword or plowshare, sheathed his ships with copper, covered his bull's-hide shield with brass, or cast lead either into pipes to convey water or into bullets to carry death, with no palace other than a hut, and no throne other than a stone, kings wore crowns of gold; while women, attired in wolf's skin, danced on the green with golden ornaments tinkling on their naked ankles. It was so in this island among the brave and hardy savages from whom we trace our descent. It was much more so in sunnier and richer lands. At the invasion of Peru, for instance, Pizarro and his Spaniards found the interior of the king's palaces adorned with the finest and most costly materials; the sides of the apartments were studded with gold and silver ornaments; their niches were filled with images of plants and animals made of the same precious metals; and even much of the domestic furniture displayed the like wanton magnificence. The Temple of the Sun shone with something of his own dazzling splendor. Every part of its interior was richly ornamented: on the eastern wall, and so situated that at his rising the rays of the sun struck directly on it, was a figure of their god, engraved on a golden plate of massive dimensions, and studded all over with emeralds and precious stones ; nor was there in that vast and splendid edifice any utensil whatever that was not made of gold or silver. Besides this, there were a hundred inferior temples in the Holy City, and many in the provinces, that almost rivaled in magnificence that of the metropolis. Historians also mention, that even the pipes which conveyed, and the fountains that contained, water in the garden of the summer palace of the Incas were of silver; and that one ornament of this fairy-like retreat consisted in full-sized imitations of foreign plants, with stalks of silver, and leaves of gold.

Where are these treasures now—the gold and silver of the world's departed empires, of such kings as Solomon, the Pharaohs of Egypt, the Cæsars of Rome, the mighty satraps and sultans of the East? They have vanished, not perished; for, while silver resists the influences that tarnish the baser metals, gold is absolutely indestructible—resisting the action of fire itself. Expose water to fire, and it dissolves in vapor; wood, and it vanishes in smoke and flame, leaving but gray ashes behind; iron, and it is converted into rust:—but fire may play on gold for a thousand years without depriving it of a degree of its lustre or an atom of its weight. Beautiful emblem of the saints of God, gold cannot perish—their trials, like the action of fire on this precious metal, but purifying what they cannot destroy.

The disappearance of the old world's treasures finds its explanation in the custom to which the man of this parable owed his fortune. In ancient times there was little trade in which men could embark, and there were no banks in which they could lodge their money.

And as secrecy offered them the best, if not only, security, it was common for people, while reserving a portion for ordinary use, to hide their gold and silver in the ground; and it often happened, through sudden death or otherwise, that the treasure was left there, their secret being buried with them. Besides this, old times were unsettled. A country was suddenly invaded,—to preserve their valuables from the hand of the spoiler, the inhabitants buried them in the earth: falling in battle or dying in exile, they never returned to claim them; and thus the earth became a bank in which was accumulated during the course of ages, a vast amount of unclaimed deposits. Even in our country, though scantily supplied with the precious metals, the spade that digs the railway, the plow that breaks up some waste moorland, is ever and anon bringing old coins to light, or still older ornaments of gold and silver. And, since the lands of the Bible were much richer than ours, and had accumulated vast stores of wealth at a period when our forefathers were naked savages, nothing was more likely to happen in these countries than the circumstance which forms the groundwork of this parable.

A peasant goes out to plow. The ground has lain undisturbed, perhaps for centuries; or, in order to recruit an exhausted soil with virgin earth, he sends his share deep into its bosom. Suddenly, as he whistles carelessly behind his oxen, he is startled by the ring of metal; and on turning his head, how he stares to see the black furrow yellow with scattered gold, and sparkling in the sun with jewels! The plow is aban-

doned; he drops on his knees;—happy man! he has lighted on an old hid treasure, and has a fortune within his grasp. Restoring the treasure to its place, he conceals with care all traces of the discovery, and, masking his joy under an air of indifference, hastens homeward. To the amazement of his neighbors, who pity him as moonstruck or mad, he sells his house, his furniture, his bed, and pulling the beds out from beneath his sleeping children, sells them—parting with all he has in the world. He is not mad, though men think so—not he. He knows what he is about. Making what others reckon a bad bargain, he purchases the field in question: and ere the villagers have recovered from their surprise, their astonishment at his folly changes to envy of his fortune. Possessor of an enormous treasure, he has exchanged a hard, humble, toiling life for the respect and ease, the comforts and luxuries, which are the eager desire of all and the happy lot of few.

Such is the incident which forms the groundwork of a parable where

THE BLESSINGS OF THE GOSPEL ARE COMPARED TO A TREASURE.

In a world which looks down on poverty, where beggars are counted offscourings, and the respect is often paid to wealth that is due only to worth, a considerable fortune will secure its possessor from contempt, and a splendid one secure his introduction to the proudest circles of the land. Yet how much higher are the rewards which the treasures of the Gospel secure to him who, though poor in this world's goods, is rich in faith? Lifting "the poor from the dust, and the needy from the dunghill to set him with princes," they introduce him to the presence of the Divine Majesty and the palace of the Great King—to the society of angels and the communion of saints—to the general assembly of those high-born and first-born, compared with whom in point of worth, or dignity, or lofty and enduring glory, your kings are but worms of the dust.

Again, if wealthy, you may reside in a splendid mansion, but it is to leave it one day for the narrow house; you may pamper the body with the costliest luxuries, but you are fattening it for worms; nor can the flashing blaze of a thousand diamonds blind our eyes to the melancholy fact that this gay, beautiful, charming form shall, stripped of all that bravery, be wrapped in a shroud, nailed up in a coffin, and thrust down into a black hole to rot. But give me the treasures of redemption, my food is manna, and my wine is love; my sweet pillow the bosom of the Son and my strong defence the arm of Almighty God; my home that palace, eternal in the heavens, where angels' harps supply the music, and woven of Jesus' righteousness the robes are fairer than angels wear. Again, the bankrupt who succeeds to a fortune is placed in circumstances to pay his debts. Is there a stain on his honor, he wipes it out; if none, he relieves himself of a load which lies heavy on the heart of an honorable man. Henceforth he neither fears to examine his accounts nor look all men in the face: and on the day when he summons his creditors to pay his debts in full, he is esteemed a happy, applauded and fêted as an honorable, man. But possessed of the treasures of the gospel, I pay debts whose sum no figures can express, nor long ages in Hell atone for; with Jesus' infinite merits I pay God all his claims; and obtaining a full discharge from the hands of Eternal Justice in the High Court of Heaven, I lift up my head, not only before men but before angels; not only in the presence of holy angels but of a holy God: and looking round on conscience and the Law, on Death and the Devil, challenge them all, saying, "It is God that justifieth, who is he that condemneth?"

A treasure! So men speak of the child who, like a beautiful flower with a worm at its root, may droop and die;—of fame won on a stage, where the spectators who applaud to-night may hiss to-morrow; of riches that, like scared wild fowl on the reedy margin of a lake, take to themselves wings and fly away. But how much worthier of the name the Friend who never leaves us; health that sickens not, and life that dies not; love that never cools, and glory that never fades; a peace that troubles may disturb but do not destroy—being to it but the raging tempest that shakes the arms of a tree which it cannot uproot; the swelling, foaming, angry billows that toss the bark which, securely anchored, they cannot part from its moorings nor dash on the surf-beaten shore!

The unspeakable value of those blessings of divine mercy, pardon, peace, and grace represented by this treasure may be tested in a simple way. In London, within whose heart there is gold in more senses of the expression than one, stands a building with armed sentinels by its door, and at its table directors with the fate of empires, with war or peace, want or plenty, in their hands. Entering by the guarded portal, and passing through the bustle of a crowded hall where Mammon sits enthroned, and gold coins are tossed about like pebbles, and silver, as in the days of Solomon, seems nothing accounted of, you descend, by strongly protected passages, to a room whose walls, divided into compartments, are formed of massive iron. Around you there are heaped, pile on pile, not thousands, but millions of money—the wealth of a great nation—the price of crowns and kingdoms. You are in the strong room of the Bank of England, one of the wonders of the world. Now, from his loom where the shuttle flies from early morn into the night, take a poor, pale-faced, but pious weaver;—from the dark mine, where any moment he may be drowned by water, blasted by fire, suffocated in the choke-damp, or buried beneath falling rocks in the bowels of the earth, take a poor begrimed, but pious pitman—and placing either in that room, offer him all its treasures on condition that he parts with that in his bosom! He would spurn the glittering bribe, saying as he returned to bless God for his brown bread and lowly home, "Get thee behind me, Satan;" or, "Thy money perish with thee!" With this blood-bought treasure he will rather die than part, saying, "It cannot be gotten for gold, neither shall silver be weighed for the price thereof; the gold and the crystal cannot equal it, and the exchange of it shall not be for jewels of pure gold; no mention shall be made of coral or of pearls, for the price of it is above rubies."

THE BLESSINGS OF THE GOSPEL ARE COMPARED TO A HID TREASURE.

The discovery of gold some years ago in our most distant colony agitated the whole kingdom; and as the news spread, thousands, breaking the ties which bound them to home, hurried away to the seaports, where crowded ships bore off the adventurers—all eagerly striving under press of sail which should first touch the happy strand. The voyage ended, our countrymen threw themselves on the gold fields; and soon the lonely dells of Australia, with emigrants from all lands, rang with the sounds of labor and a Babel of tongues. Yet long years before its treasures were brought to light, shepherds had left our hills to herd the flock on Australia's boundless pastures: the hut of the squatter had encroached on the hunting-grounds, and his axe had sounded in the forests of the wondering savage; and there, earning only a bare subsistence, far removed from the homes and friends of their love, without hope of improving their condition or returning with a fortune, many had pined and drooped—like a flower removed from its native to an uncongenial soil. Yet all the while a fortune lay hid beneath the exile's feet; the roots of the tree under whose shadow he reclined, recalling scenes and friends far away, were matting rocks of gold; and from the bed of the stream where he quenched his thirst, thousands, with thirst for gold burning as his, came afterwards to draw splendid fortunes,—vaulting at once from abject poverty to the heights of affluence. He lived poor in the midst of riches; and daily walking above wealth that had made him independent of labor, he sank, exhausted by toil and care and sad regrets, into an early and lonely grave. Such fate befell many a one, with gold enough in the stones that formed his rude hearth, or in the rock against which his log-hut stood, to surround him with the splendors of a brilliant fortune.

Now that poor man, with his ragged tent pitched on a gold field, but ignorant of the treasure which he might have possessed and enjoyed, is the type and image of thousands. The treasures of the Gospel, they, as he had those of gold, have and yet have not. They are hid from them. Their minds, as Paul says, are blinded—"The God of this world hath blinded the minds of them which believe not."—"The natural man receiveth not the things of the Spirit of God, for they are foolishness unto him; neither can he know them, because they are spiritually discerned." Were God to make these treasures as plain to men as the plowshare did this to the peasant's wondering, rejoicing, sparkling eyes, they would leave the house of God for their homes happier far than he. What is gold to these? Within the two boards of the poor man's Bible is a greater wealth of happiness, of honor, of pleasure, of true peace, than Australia hides in the gold of all her mines. That, for example, could not buy the pardon of any of the thousand criminals whom a country, weary of their crimes, once cast on her distant shores; but here is what satisfies a justice stricter than man's, and procures the forgiveness of sins which the stoutest heart may tremble to think of. Again, the wealth of the most successful adventurer cannot conceal the meanness of his birth, give polish to his manners, or raise him to a level with an ancient and jealous nobility: it alters the condition, but not the character of the man; and associated with ignorance, meanness, vulgarity, is, to use the figure of the wise man, only as "a jewel in a swine's snout." But, accompanied with the blessing from on high and received into the heart by faith, the Gospel alters both our character and condition—making the rude gentle, the coarse refined, the impure holy, the selfish generous—working a greater transformation than if a felon of the prison were to change into a courtier of the palace, or the once ragged boy who had been educated to crime on the streets were to wear a star on his manly breast and stand in the brilliant circle that surrounds a throne. In the blood of Christ to wash out sin's darkest stains, in the grace of God to purify the foulest heart, in peace to calm life's roughest storms, in hopes to cheer guilt's darkest hour, in a courage that defies death and descends calmly into the tomb, in that which makes the poorest rich and without which the richest are poor indeed, the Gospel

——— has treasures greater far
Than east or west unfold,
And its rewards more precious are
Than all their stores of gold.

THE TREASURE WAS FOUND WITHOUT BEING SOUGHT.

Each spring which by the voices of birds breaking the long winter silence, reminds us that other voices, now mute, shall wake again, and by the flowers on the green sod above our dead, reminds us that they also shall rise again—beautiful from dust, immortal from the bed of mortality, is emblematical of conversion as well as of resurrection. It is Christ's own voice speaking through the Spirit to souls for love of whom he left the skies, which I recognize in this beautiful and tender address, "Rise up, my love, my fair one, and come away. For, lo, the winter is past; the rain is over and gone; the flowers appear on the earth; the time of the singing of birds is come; the voice of the turtle is heard in the land; the fig-tree putteth forth her green figs: and the vines with the tender grape give a smell. Arise, my love, my fair one, and come away." In new life, life as from the dead, in songs of love, smiling skies and balmy air, budding woods and fields which hold the seeds of future, golden, bountiful harvests, the spring is an emblem worthy of conversion—the fitting dress of so great an event.

Besides, both in trees and flowers the spring presents remarkable illustrations of that variety with which God is pleased to work in saving souls, and turning sinners from the error of their ways. All his people are converted; must be so—for our Lord says, "Except a man be born again he cannot see the kingdom of God." But all are not converted in the selfsame manner; and there are in grace, as in nature, to use

Paul's words, " diversities of operations, but it is the same God which worketh all in all." For example, the leaves of roses, of tulips, and of our orchard fruit-trees appear first—preparing the way for flowers still in the bud. In other cases this order is reversed. In the catkins of the hoary willow hung on naked stems, in the gold and silver cups of the crocus, whether they spring from the grass of Alpine meadows or edge our parterres with a beautiful border, the flowers precede the leaves—these plants, like a day unheralded by a dawn, burst into blossom without any apparent preparation. Even so, while some after a long search for true happiness and their souls' good, in fulfillment of the promise, "seek and ye shall find," get in Jesus Christ the treasure of this parable and the pearl of the next, others find a Saviour without seeking him. They burst at once into a state of grace; and without seeking, or so much as thinking of it, they stumble on salvation, if I may say so, as this man on the treasure hid in the field. They are converted, and it is a great surprise to them—what neither they nor any one else expected.

Ambitious of riches and yet averse to work, men have resorted to necromancy to discover hidden treasures, digging for them in fields and amid hoary ruins. The man whose good-fortune is recorded here was otherwise employed. Bred up in poverty, and satisfied with his lot—the robust health of out-door occupation, an appetite that gave zest to the plainest fare, the lively prattle of his children when he came home at even, he thought no more of riches than some of conversion, who, suddenly changed, rise in the morning in a state of nature and close the day in a state of grace. His good-fortune, if I may say so, was an accident—the merest accident; and thereby distinguished from the case of him who found the pearl of great price. He, a merchant seeking goodly pearls, found what he sought; but this man what he was not seeking, nor even so much as thinking of.

Equally different are the cases of those whom a God, sovereign in working as he is great in mercy, converts to a saving knowledge of the truth. For example, Nicodemus, who repaired to Christ under the cloud of night, was one seeking goodly pearls; so also was the centurion, who "was a just man and one that feared God," and to whom Peter was sent with the tidings of a Saviour; and so in some sense also was that unhappy youth who with more courage than Nicodemus came in open day, and pushing his way through the crowd, thus accosted our Lord, "Good master, what shall I do to inherit eternal life?"—only when Jesus told him to sell all, give the price to the poor, and follow him, he judged the terms too hard, the cost too great. Like many others he sought the pearl but disliked the price. On the other hand, showing that God will have mercy on whom he will have mercy, and that salvation is of grace and not of merit, he sometimes bestows it where it has never been sought; and a change comes as unlooked for as in the case of Saul, the son of Kish—leaving home to seek his father's asses he found a crown on the road, and he who went out a commoner came back a king. Look, for instance, at the case of Zaccheus! Curiosity to see Jesus draws him from the receipt of custom; and leaving his books and money bags—for he was rich, he throws himself into the crowd. In vain the little publican stands on tip-toe. He can see nothing. Leaving the throng behind, he hies away; and climbing a friendly sycamore that threw its branches over the road, he perches himself on a bough, proud of his ingenuity and congratulating himself on the excellent view he will command as Jesus passes—borne along on the crest of popular favor. His curiosity once gratified, he has no purpose other than of returning to his old habits and resuming the pursuit of gain. What he sought he found; but more, in that, besides a sight of the Saviour, he obtained a hold of salvation. Jesus, as he passed by, looked up, and calling him down, invited himself to his house; and ere nightfall there was a greater transformation wrought on that poor worldling than appears in the insect which lies coffined in the morning within its narrow cell, and ere sunset is roaming on wide-spread wings from flower to flower—its bed their cups, its food their honied nectar. Another instance of people obtaining salvation who were not seeking it, is found in that Samaritan who after long years of sin, is sitting crowned like a queen in heaven. With pitcher poised on her head, she leaves her village to draw water,—having no other purpose than to prepare a meal for her paramour on his return from the labors of the day. Shading her eyes from the glare of the sun, she descries a lone traveler resting on Jacob's well. The man and she meet; they converse;

and she who had approached the well with the slow step and graceful carriage of Eastern women, leaving both it and her pitcher, hurries back with eager eyes and flying feet. What has happened? She has found her Saviour—found, as she said, "the Christ;" and at the news the whole village,—mothers with infants at the breast and old age bending on its staff,—leave looms silent and streets deserted to see Jesus.

Even so, it may happen that some who repair to the house of God without any expectation or even wish to be converted, and with no better purpose than to see or be seen, may there behold a sight they never expected, and meet one whom they looked not for. Drawn to the church only by curiosity to hear some preacher, they may, Zaccheus-like, receive a call from the preacher's master; and so the scene of an idle curiosity may be turned into that of a true conversion. There are some cases in which God has made even the wrath of man to praise him—those who went to mock having stayed to pray. Let me give an example. A stranger to the congregation was one day preaching in a church in England. He wound up an impressive sermon by telling them that, some twenty years before, three bad young men had entered that very house with the intention of stoning the minister. Something, a look or word from the preacher, led one of the three to hesitate. In consequence of this the plot was abandoned: and while his associates who were angry with him for his pusillanimity left the scene, he lingered behind from no other motive than curiosity. The preacher went on to tell how one of the two who left was, some few years afterwards, guilty of a horrid murder, and hanged for it; and how the other also for some other crime ended his life on the gallows. As to the third who stayed behind, strange to say, he was converted on that occasion, and afterwards became a minister of the gospel; and, the preacher added, his voice trembling the while with ill-suppressed emotion, He now addresses you in me—a monument of the grace of God, a brand plucked from the burning. And since, as that case proves, God's grace is sovereign, and Jesus is the same yesterday, to-day, and to-morrow, of whom may we not hope? The pardon of all our sins through the blood of the Lamb of God, the sanctifying influences of his Holy Spirit, glory for a crown and heaven for a home, these, like the treasures which the plowshare brought to light, lie at our feet. They are within our reach. And why, if yet poor and miserable, with no better portion than a passing, perishing world, should not we stoop down to make them our own; and saved, through God's free grace and sovereign mercy, be of those of whom it is said, "He was found of them who sought him not"?

THE CONDUCT OF THE FINDER.

He hid the treasure.—"It is naught, it is naught, saith the buyer;" and though this man may not have depreciated the real, he took pains to conceal the accidental value of the field. We are not required to settle such questions of moral casuistry as the method he took to possess himself of this treasure may suggest. To the profits of such discoveries as are the fruits of a man's observation or inventive genius, our law gives him the exclusive right—at least for a term of years; nor would it regard the profits of this discovery as belonging of right to the proprietor of the soil. In this country, *treasure-trove*, as it is called, is claimed by the crown. But whether this man's conduct was justifiable is not a question we are called to settle. In hiding the treasure till he had made himself owner of the field, he took the surest way of making it his own, and expressed, better than any words could do, its value in his eyes. Teaching us how to act in those matters that belong to salvation, he spared no pains, and lost not an hour, and grudged no sacrifice to possess himself of this treasure—and, as applied to the infinitely more valuable treasures of the gospel, these are the points which Jesus proposes for our imitation. By this parable the Saviour calls men to leave no stone unturned, no pains untaken, no anxiety unfelt, no prayer unsaid, no Sabbath nor day unimproved to make these treasures theirs. And, O, how happy the wretched, how calm the troubled, how cheerful the sad, how pure the foulest, how rich the poorest, in view of death how brave the timid, in death itself how tranquil, even triumphant, all might be, if we only felt as much concern and took as much care to find Christ, as this man to secure a fleeting treasure.

Unless in the sense of guarding their peace of mind from being disturbed by temptation, and their purity from being stained by sin, those who find treasures in the Gospel, do not hide them. On the contrary, they seek to make the great discovery known, and to communicate its benefits to all. There is no temptation to do otherwise, to keep it to ourselves, since it has blessings in the pardon and peace of God enough for us and for all others. It is as if one of a caravan that had sunk on the burning desert, were, in making a last effort for life, to discover no muddy pool, but a vast fountain—cool as the snows that replenished its spring, and pure as the heavens that were reflected on its bosom. He revives at the blessed sight, and, pushing on to the margin, stoops to drink; yet ere his thirst is fully quenched, see how he speeds away to pluck his friends from the arms of death; and, hark! how he shouts, making the lone desert ring to the cry, "Ho, every one that thirsteth, come ye to the waters." None ever found Christ but they wished that others also might find him, were ever saved without a desire to save springing up in their hearts—theirs the spirit of Andrew, when he went to his brother Peter, crying, "We have found the Messias,"—of those who said "Come thou with us, we will do thee good," "Arise, for we have seen the land, and behold it is very good."

HE PARTS WITH ALL FOR THIS TREASURE.

On boating once along a coast where the billows roared in the deep caves, and broke in sheets of foam on the face of cliffs that rose hundreds of feet sheer up from the sea, we heard the sound of merry voices mingling with the sea-mew's screams; and on looking up saw to our surprise a group of urchins standing with their backs against the rocky wall, and with scant room on its projecting ledges for their naked feet. One false step, a dizzy moment, and the body, bounding from ledge to ledge, had sunk like lead into the deep. Yet these children, poised on the beetling crag, were light-hearted as any culling the flowers of the meadow, or sitting by their mother's side on the hearth of the fisherman's hut. Their safety lay in this, that they had been reared among such scenes, and accustomed from early infancy to positions that would have turned our heads. On the other hand a sudden elevation is usually followed by a sudden fall; and such is the danger he is exposed to, who, like the man of this parable, is raised by one rapid revolution of the wheel of fortune from great poverty to great affluence. The man gets intoxicated with joy; the head grows giddy; and falling into habits of boundless extravagance, or, worse still, into habits of profligacy and vice, he is ruined—his fortune proving in the end a great misfortune. So imminent indeed is this danger, that there is no wise and prudent pious father but would tremble for his boy, should he, when preparing himself to fight his way on in life, suddenly succeed to the possession of a fortune.

In the treasures of gold and silver there lurks great danger; in those of grace none: nor is there a good man but would rejoice should his son come, with beaming face, to announce the tidings that he had found a Saviour; pardon and grace and peace in Jesus Christ.

Unlike common riches, this treasure breeds neither jealousies nor fears nor envy. No Christian woman repines that her husband loves Jesus better than her:

no godly mother, however she may feel the pang of parting, but approves the son who, burning with love to souls, tears himself from her arms to plant the cross on heathen shores. Your families of noble blood or ancient pedigree eye him with jealousy who, emerging from the obscurity of humble life, rises with his plebeian blood to a position lofty as their own. But next to the joy of possessing the treasures and honors of the Gospel is that of seeing poor sinners made heirs of the grace of God, and heaven's highest titles bestowed on those that were the vilest of mankind. The greater the number who get this treasure, the greater the joy of those who already have it. And how great and deep that joy, is set forth in the conduct of this man—he parted with all he had to possess the treasure. What he paid indeed was not the value of it; and certainly this parable was not told to teach us that when the haughty part with their pride, and drunkards with their cup, the licentious with their vices, the gay with their vanities, the avaricious with the love of money, others with their darling sins, they thereby purchase salvation. Assuredly not. Salvation is all of grace. Yet these things are required.—"Let him that nameth the name of Christ depart from all iniquity."—"Whosoever would be my disciple, let him take up his cross, deny himself daily and follow me." "Ye cannot," says our Lord, "serve God and Mammon." Shrink not from the pain these sacrifices must cost. It is not so great as many fancy. The joy of the Lord is his people's strength. Love has so swallowed up all sense of pain, and sorrow been so lost in ravishment, that men of old took joyfully the spoiling of their goods, and martyrs went to the burning stake with beaming countenances, and sang high death-songs amid the roaring flames. Let us by faith rise above the world, and it will shrink into littleness and insignificance compared with Christ. Some while ago two aeronauts, hanging in mid-air, looked down on the earth from their balloon, and wondered to see how small great things had grown—ample fields were contracted into little patches—the lake was no bigger than a looking-glass—the broad river with ships floating on its bosom, seemed like a silver snake—the wide-spread city was reduced to the dimensions of a village—the long, rapid, flying train appeared but a black caterpillar slowly creeping over the surface of the ground. And such changes the world undergoes to the eyes of him who, rising to hold communion with God and anticipating the joys of heaven, lives above it and looks beyond it. This makes it easy and even joyful to part with all for Christ—this is the victory that overcometh the world, even our faith.

VIII.
The Parable of the Pearl of Great Price.

Matthew xiii. 45, 46.

THE costliest jewel mentioned by ancient writers is a pearl which belonged to Cleopatra, the beautiful but infamous queen of Egypt; and the strongest proof which Roman historians have to give of the wanton and boundless extravagance of some of their emperors is the fact that they dissolved pearls in vinegar, and drank them with their wine. In harmony with these passages of profane history, this and other parts of sacred Scripture prove that among jewels the highest place in former times was assigned to pearls. When our Lord, for example, warned his disciples to beware how they wasted truths of the highest value on such as could not appreciate them, he selects these as their emblem, saying, "Give not that which is holy unto dogs, neither cast ye your pearls before swine." Such place also pearls hold in the attire of the woman whom John names "Mystery, Babylon the Great, the mother of harlots and abominations of the earth, who was drunken with the blood of the saints, and with the blood of the martyrs of Jesus." In a picture, so graphic as to remind us of the memorable words of Lord Bacon—who said that, if the descriptions of Antichrist were extracted from Scripture and put into the *Hue and Cry*, there was not a constable in all England but would apprehend the Pope,—John describes the dress as well as the deeds of this bloody persecutor. She was arrayed, he says, "in purple and scarlet color, and decked with gold and precious stones and pearls;" and here, be it observed, while other gems, however beautiful and costly,—the flashing diamond, and burning ruby, and purple amethyst, and sea-green emerald, and sapphire with hues borrowed from the sky,—are only mentioned under the general term of precious stones, pearls, as more valuable than these, are distinctly named. From all which we are warranted to conclude that when our Lord compared "the kingdom of heaven," the blessings, in other words, of redeeming love, to "one pearl of great price," he intended to set them forth as of pre-eminent value; as in fact, amid a thousand things desirable, the one thing needful.

But, besides its money value, a pearl such as this presented a remarkable as well as beautiful emblem of salvation in other aspects—in, for instance, a color of snowy whiteness, a purity unclouded by the slightest haze, and a form so round and polished and perfect that it was impossible to improve it. The lapidary, to whose grinding skill the very diamond owes much of its brilliancy and those many-colored fires with which it shines and burns, may not touch a pearl. His art cannot add to its beauty—the polish of its snowy surface, or the perfection of its rounded form. And what an emblem, therefore, is this gem of that salvation which came perfect from the hand of God—of that righteousness of Jesus Christ which, as no guilt of ours can stain, no works of ours can improve—of that Gospel which, as revealed in the Bible, is without defect of truth or admixture of error, and which the last of the inspired writers therefore closes with this solemn warning: "If any man shall add unto these things, God shall add unto him the plagues that are written in this book: and if any man shall take away from the words of the book of this prophecy, God shall take away his part out of the book of life, and out of the holy city."

Nor does this pearl present an emblem of salvation in respect only of its incalculable price and intrinsic characters. In the hazards and sacrifices at which both were obtained, we discern, however faintly, another point of resemblance. Other gems, the diamond and ruby and emerald and sapphire, lie bedded in river-courses, or set in the solid rocks; and there men seek them without loss of health or risk of life. But pearls belong to the ocean; they are gems which she casts not up among the pebbles that strew her beach, but hides in her dangerous and darkest depths. Hence a dreadful trade is the pearl-fisher's. Weighted with stone to sink him, and inhaling a long, deep-drawn breath, he leaps from the boat's side, and, the parting waves closing above his head, descends into the depths of the sea to grope for the shelly spoils amid the dim light which faintly illuminates her slimy bed; nor rises, breathless and black in face, to the surface till on-lookers have begun to fear that he will rise no more. And not unfrequently he never does. These waters are the haunts of terrible monsters; and, marked for its prey by the swift and fierce and voracious shark, in vain the wretched man stirs the muddy bottom to raise a cloud to cover his escape. Some air-bells bubbling up, and blood that spreads crimsoning the surface of the sea, are all that is evermore seen of one who dies a sacrifice to his hazardous pursuits; and the story of the dangers which pearl-fishers have always to encounter, and the dreadful deaths they have often to endure, will recall to a reflective mind the memory of Him who, in salvation, purchased this pearl at so great a price—giving his life for ours, and dying, the just for the unjust, that he might bring us to God.

Though it belongs to ages long gone by, I may mention another aspect of this emblem that devout men once considered peculiarly appropriate. Ere the progress of science had robbed this and other things of their wonders, they saw in the manner in which the pearl was said to be generated a figure of the mystery of our Lord's divine descent and miraculous conception. Unlike those which are found in the womb of the dead earth, this gem is formed within the shell of a living creature; and in old times it was believed that when the heavens were in a peculiar state, manifesting their activity in flashes of lightning and peals of thunder, the future parent of the pearl rose from the bottom to the surface of the sea, and, opening its shelly mouth, received something of the nature of a dewdrop from the propitious skies. From this germ, with which the shell-fish descended again into its native depths, the pearl was believed to be formed; and in this natural mystery and strange birth of the precious gem, old divines saw an emblem of our Lord's descent into the dark humiliations of this lower world, the overshadowing of the Holy Ghost, and the conception of the Virgin's womb. The researches of naturalists have taught us that the pearl has no claim to such a lofty and heavenly descent. Yet, though science has robbed that as well as many things else of the dignity which belongs to the mysterious, and pearls now-a-days have lost much of their pre-eminent value, neither the discoveries of science, nor the changes of time and fashion, have abated the value or lessened the wonders of redeeming love. Jesus is the same yesterday, to-day, and forever: and salvation, with its blood-bought and inestimable blessings, will ever remain that "one pearl of great price" which may be found by all; and which whosoever finds should sell all he has to buy,—saying, with the apostle, "I count all things but loss that I may win Christ."

In opening up this parable let us consider

THE PERSONS REPRESENTED BY THIS MERCHANT.

Mankind present all shades of color,—from the negro, God's image in ebony, as one said, to the fair-skinned, blue-eyed, golden-haired types of our Scandinavian ancestors,—all varieties also of disposition, from the penuriousness of Nabal to the affection embalmed by David in this immortal song: "I am distressed for thee, my brother Jonathan: very pleasant hast thou been unto me: thy love to me was wonderful, passing the love of women,"—all degrees also of sense, from the fool who, untaught by experience, though pounded in a mortar comes out the same, to those astute, far-seeing, and long-headed men, whose utterances, like the counsels of Ahitophel, are "as if a man inquired at the oracle of God,"—and all differences also of outward condition, from Lazarus covered with sores and clothed in rags nor ever enjoying one good full meal, upward to him who, clothed in purple and fine linen, fares sumptuously every day. Yet in God's sight the whole human family is divisible into two classes, and only two—the good and bad, the chaff and wheat, the wheat and tares, the sheep and goats, the converted and the unconverted—those that, still at enmity with God, lie under condemnation, and such as, renewed in the spirit of their minds and reconciled to Him by the blood of his Son, are in a state of grace.

But, like those great orders of plants or animals which we meet with in the sciences of botany and zoology, these two classes are divisible into numerous subdivisions, differing apparently, though not radically, so much from each other that some sinners seem to stand more nearly related to saints than to many of their own class; just as, for instance, the sponge or branching coral, fixed to the rocks and belonging to the animal kingdom, looks more allied to the tangle that sways than to the fishes that swim in the flowing tide. Let no man therefore conclude that he must be converted because there are broad outward marks of difference between him and many who certainly are not. People have gone down to hell, as the Pharisee did to his house, thanking God that they are not as others. The difference between them has been more apparent than real, being no greater than that between two nights—one where the bark seems to sail in the moonshine on a silver sea, and the other so pitchy dark that her outlook can see neither coast nor reef, though he hears the roar of breakers; or between two bodies both dead—one still beautiful in death, and the other a horrid spectacle of loathsome and ghastly decay. In such circumstances how necessary it is to remember our Saviour's warning: "Take heed that ye be not deceived." What though we are seeking even goodly pearls, unless we have found the one of great price?

And there are such people. Owing to the influence of a pious education, or of something naturally elevated and refined in their disposition, or of the society in which they move, or of some more mysterious causes, there are people in the world, and of the world too, who may be said to be seeking goodly pearls. They cultivate refined enjoyments; they are pursuing patriotic and philanthropic objects; they are seeking to be good, and to do good; they feel that man's happiness cannot lie in gratifications which satisfy the brutes, or in empty gaiety, or in the common prizes of ambition, or in any amount of money, but in nobler and godlike pursuits—in purity of heart, peace of conscience, and that happy relationship to God without which there is no more rest for a human soul than there was for the wandering dove till, skimming the waters on drooping wing, she returned to her home in the ark. These are "not far from the kingdom of heaven;" and were in it, would they take but another step. Almost Christians, they are almost saved. But what avails it to have almost made the port? So did the ship whose naked timbers I once passed sticking out of the water. Struck by a giant sea, she stove in her sides on the point of the pier, and went to pieces in the harbor's mouth; and as on entering it I passed these skeleton ribs bedded in the sand below and rising on the tide above, they had a warning look, and seemed to say, that as in that case so in the case of souls, "almost saved" was but another expression for "altogether lost."

Let it be observed that different characters, different classes of sinners, are represented as being saved in the two parables of the Hid Treasure and the Pearl of Great Price. For examples of these, let me select two remarkable men—Colonel Gardiner and John Bunyan. Gardiner's was a sudden and remarkable conversion. Previous to that, he, who afterwards proved himself as brave as soldier of the Cross as of an earthly sovereign on that fatal field where, refusing to fly, he fell beneath the Highlander's scythe, was a mere man of the world —not a lover only of pleasure, but of the basest pleasures. The eventful night which he so unexpectedly passed in prayer, he had intended to spend in the arms of sin. As he impatiently watched the finger of the clock moving slowly on to the hour of a guilty assignation, nothing was further from his thoughts than conversion; and had Death himself, throwing open the chamber door, stood before him in visible form, he had not been more startled than by the blow, dealt by an unseen hand, which laid him penitent at the feet of Jesus. In salvation Gardiner found as much as the man in the treasure which his plowshare brought to light, what he neither sought nor expected. In Bunyan, on the other hand, we see one who had come to know that the world and its pleasures could never satisfy the cravings of his heart. He felt the need of being other than he was. As an imprisoned eagle, chained to its perch and turning its eye up to the blue heavens, feels the strivings of a native instinct, and springing upwards beats the bars of its cage with bleeding wings, Bunyan tried to rise out of his estate of sin and misery. He made vigorous efforts to keep the law of God—to live without sin—to establish a righteousness of his own—to work out a sum of merits, and thereby obtain peace and pardon, and reconcile himself to God. Seeking the pardon of sin, a purer life, and a holier heart, he had been a merchant seeking "goodly pearls." And as in his case the seeker became the finder, so shall all who, like him, listen to the voice of Jesus, saying, "Turn ye, turn ye—I am the way, the truth, the life—all which your souls need and your hearts desire is found in me, 'the one pearl' —for whosoever believeth in me shall not perish, but have everlasting life."

THE PEARL OF GREAT PRICE.

Wealth in our country is measured by the amount of money which a man has lodged in bank or afloat in business, the value of his house and its furnishings, or the number of acres in his estate. It is quite different in many parts of the East. There you enter a house with walls of clay and thatch of straw or reeds or palm-leaves, and in its tenant—who sits, simply attired and amid the scantiest funiture, cross-legged on a rug which, spread out on the naked floor, forms his seat by day and his bed by night—you find a man of enormous wealth. He has it invested in jewels—nor without reason. In countries liable, on the one hand, to sudden invasion, and on the other to sudden and violent revolutions, where bloody tyrants oppress their subjects, and wealth is the carcase that draws the eagles together, it is in the form of jewels that property is most securely because most secretly kept, and in the case of flight most easily removed. Here, for example, is a family who, with villages in flames behind them, are flying from a ruined home and wretched country. They seek safety elsewhere; and, with nothing saved but their scanty clothing, seem reduced to the greatest want. Yet stop the mother who carries one child on her breast and has another at her side, and, undoing her raven locks, shake them out, and a shower of diamonds falls at your feet. In this form, and hid in a woman's hair, fortunes have often been carried from place to place in the East; and it is only by taking this fact into account, that while with us little else than ornaments, precious stones are there a form of money, and often of immense wealth, we rise to an adequate idea of the value which Christ puts on his people in calling them his jewels; or of the full meaning of a figure that represents the blessings of his salvation, as "one pearl of great price" which all other pearls and property should be sold to buy.

As all which the merchant sought in acquiring many goodly pearls was found in one—one precious, peerless gem, Jesus teaches us that the soul finds in himself all it feels the want of, and has been seeking in other ways—peace with God and peace of conscience, a clean heart and a renewed mind, comfort in sorrow and a sweet satisfaction with all the discipline of providence, hope in death and a heaven of glory after it. Great as are these blessings in respect of their value, they are equally so in respect of their price. They cost God's only Son long years of the deepest humiliation—his bloody agony and dreadful death; and yet, alas! in being offered to sinners who despise and reject Him, how often is this pearl cast before swine? To them who believe, Christ is precious; but what can be more sad than to see the value a woman sets on trinkets, the pride with which she shows and wears her jewels, while Jesus has no preciousness in her eyes? What fools people are! They set more on some glittering bits of glass or stone than on a crown of glory!—they care more in this dying body for the perishable casket than for the immortal jewel which it holds! Can a maid forget her ornaments, or a bride her attire? Yet my people, says God, have forgotten me days without number. From such sin and folly, good Lord preserve us!

HOW THIS PEARL WAS OBTAINED.

It was not bestowed as a gift. On the contrary, this merchantman, trading in goodly pearls, bought it at the price of all he had. If so, where, it may be asked, lies the analogy between this case and a salvation that, all of mercy and not at all of merit, is the free gift of God through Jesus Christ our Lord? In answer to that question, let it be observed, that the Bible has paradoxes—things that appear contradictory, destructive as fire and water are of each other; and yet are true. We have a living one, if I may say so, in our Lord himself. He is a creature, and yet the Creator—he is the Son of man, and yet the Son of God—he is the victim of death, and yet his victor—he is the captive of the grave, and yet her spoiler—he is Lord of all, and yet, with water and towel in hand, he stoops as the lowest servant to wash his servant's feet—there on Calvary's bloody cross he suffers as a man, and yet saves as a God. And Christ's followers, like himself, present to a wondering world what seems inconsistent features, impossible combinations. Are they not, to quote Paul's words, unknown, and yet well known—dying, and behold we live—chastened, and not killed—sorrowful, yet always rejoicing—poor, yet making many rich—having nothing, and yet possessing all things? Now as—though people may ask, how can these things be?—both are true, it is as true that salvation is a free gift, and yet a thing to be bought and sold. Nay, more and stranger still, it is bought "without money and without price." A trader with-

out either money or credit has no footing in the markets where Mammon presides, and man is the seller as well as the buyer; but in the market which Divine Mercy opens, and over which Divine Love presides, and where "gold tried in the fire," and robes washed in the blood of the Lamb, and celestial crowns all set with gems of glory are displayed, wealth and character offer no advantage. Here the poor get as good bargains as the rich—often better indeed; harlots and publicans enter the kingdom, while scribes and pharisees are left standing at the door.

I do not mean to disparage good works. Christians are to be careful to maintain them, and to "make their light so to shine before men that they, seeing their good works, may glorify their Father which is in heaven." But we are on the wrong road altogether if we are attempting to earn or deserve salvation by these. No gathered sum of human merits, of virtues, prayers, or charities can, like the accumulation of money that forms the price of an estate, purchase heaven. We have to buy, no doubt,—but not after the world's fashion. The price, on the contrary, which we are required to pay is not virtues and merits, but just that we abandon all trust in these; give up in them what we may have reckoned goodly pearls; and consent to be saved as poor, lost, undone sinners—whose type is the beggar that, clad in filthy rags and knocking timidly at our door, stands before us, making no appeal but to our compassion, and urging no plea whatever but our mercy and his own great misery. Still, though we cannot, in the ordinary sense of the term, buy salvation, no man is saved but he who gives up his sins for Christ—takes up his cross, and, denying himself daily, follows Jesus. We are not saved in sin, but *from* it; and, though we cannot buy salvation, we are to seek it as those who, if they could, would buy it at any price, at any pain—giving the whole world, were it theirs, for Christ; and as earnestly seeking and as highly esteeming Him as she who exclaimed: "Were I on one bank of a river and saw Jesus on the other, and that river ran burning fire, I would dash into the flames to reach Him."

SOME LESSONS TAUGHT BY THIS FIGURE OF A MERCHANT.

When Napoleon Bonaparte, after subduing Europe, found himself unable to subdue us, and saw his armies broken on our firm front like waves which the storm launches against a rocky headland, he called us, in his impotent rage, "a nation of shopkeepers." Owing our power and wealth more to commerce than to anything else, in a sense we are so—nor are we ashamed of being so. Trade is an honorable occupation. Like those ocean streams that temper the cold of northern climes with the heat of the tropics, and float ice-field and iceberg southward to cool the air of the torrid zone, its currents also convey to different lands the peculiar blessings of each; and, besides thus binding country to country in the bonds of mutual advantage, it promises to be an instrument in the providence of God of diffusing the blessings of Christianity over the world. A nation of traders whose merchants are princes, and whose traffickers are the honorable of the earth, there is no figure in the Bible—neither that of a shepherd, nor of a soldier, nor of a watchman, nor of a husbandman, nor of a householder—which comes more home to us than that of a merchant. It suggests many lessons; and to select a few of them I remark that—

It teaches us to make religion our chief pursuit.— Such is to the merchant his business. To it he does not allot merely some hours stolen from the pursuits of pleasure. He rises to business every morning; it engages his entire attention during the day; nor, save during a few hours in the evening, and a few days, or weeks at most, in the year, does he ever yield himself up to the enjoyments of ease. In its pursuit he is all energy and activity. What a hold it takes of his mind!—forming the topic of his conversation at feasts, and often at funerals—intruding itself unbidden, and to a good man unwelcome into the closet where he prays and the church where he worships!

Would God that the business of eternity had as strong a hold of our minds! But, alas! the least thing puts it out of our head. And what greater contrast than the appearance of the same people in a church and at a market—the dull worshipers of this scene and the keen traders of that—the listless aspect of the Sabbath congregation and the animated looks of the market crowd! Enter an auction-mart, what life, what keen competitors, what watching to catch a chance!—no sleepers there, but every face turned up to him who, raised above the eager crowd, descants on the bargains to be had. Enter a church, and how different the aspect of many?—people asleep in the pews—listlessness in the countenances and weariness in the attitudes of others. Who would believe this to be a crowd of men under sentence of death, whom one is telling how to break their chains and escape the gallows—a crowd gathered on the deck and hanging over the bulwarks of a sinking ship, whom one who has brought a life-boat to the scene, is offering to rescue from the roaring waves and a dreadful doom? The danger there is that, unless you back your oars and go warily to work, the eager throng, rushing *en masse* to the side and throwing themselves headlong in, will swamp your boat; but, alas! the chances in that church are, that not one of a hundred, or one of a thousand, accepts the offer. If I may use a common expression, multitudes make religion a *bye-job*, and not a business,—giving it but the ends and odds of time; and many not even that. May God help us to throw our whole heart into this business; teaching us to give all diligence to make our calling and election sure—to work out our salvation with fear and trembling—to work while it is called to-day, seeing that the night cometh when no man can work!

It teaches us to guard against deception.—The money which has a suspicious look the wary trader rings on his counter; knowing what frauds are practised in business, the wise merchant often puts such goods as he receives to the test; and the utmost care is taken in such a trade especially as that of this parable to guard against mistakes or imposition. Before buying a gem, the jewel-merchant examines it with a powerful magnifier—nor without reason. The smallest speck on a diamond detracts greatly from its value: worthless bits of glass are so cut and colored as to pass for precious stones: and by means of the brilliant scales of a small fish which inhabits a river in France, they fabricate such perfect imitations of the pearl, as to impose on ordinary, and almost to deceive the quickest, eyes. The dupes of fraud, men have paid immense sums for pearls which were found to be only paste.

But, through the deceitfulness of the heart and wiles of the devil, men have been greater dupes and suffered unspeakably greater losses. As it is not all gold that glitters, it is not all grace that seems so. There is a counterfeit peace as well as counterfeit coin—there are hopes of heaven which rest on sand as well as hopes founded on the Rock of Ages—there is a righteousness which is ours, as well as one which is Christ's—there are virtues that, like sweet wild-flowers, cling to the ruins of humanity as well as graces that are the fruit of the Holy Spirit—there are kind and generous, but merely natural, as well as holy and heavenly affections. Such being the case, no merchant needs to be more on his guard against fraud and deception than those who may flatter themselves that they are regenerated when they are only reformed. Many, it is to be feared, fancy that they are on the way to heaven who are on the way to hell; that they are at peace with God when their only peace is that of the river which is locked in ice—the quiet and silence of a tomb where there is no disturbance just because there is death!

It teaches us to examine our accounts with God.— There is a biography called "The Successful Merchant," and, without having read it, I will venture to affirm that Budgett—this merchant—was careful to balance his books, and apply to his business the spirit of the Apostle's precept, "Let a man examine himself." Alas! that in the use of such a precaution the children of this world should be so much wiser than the children of light! It is a part of every merchant's education to learn that art; and it is his only safety to practise it. Neglecting to balance his books, he may launch out into expenses quite unsuitable to his circumstances; persevere in branches of business which are not to his profit, but loss; fancy he is making money when he is driving on ruin. No other fate awaits the reckless adventurer than that of the emigrant ship which some weeks ago, with hundreds on board of her, full of hopes of happiness and fortune in the New World, ran headlong on Cape Race to break in pieces, and, whelming its living freight into the devouring waves, gave them a grave on the shores where they expected a happy home! They took no soundings, and so they found no safety. The wise merchant takes stock, balances his books, and, in some businesses at least, strikes a balance on every day's transactions. In this, as in the energy and toil and self-denial and resolution of worldly, how much is there worthy of the imitation of Christian, men? Why should not we, at the close of each day, recall and review its transactions to see how our accounts stand with conscience and with God—what duties had been neglected, and what done—what temptations had been resisted, and what yielded to; how far we had indulged evil passions, how far mortified them—how like or how unlike to Christ's our demeanor had been? This were a scrutiny which, though often painful and humbling, would be attended with the happiest results. How many sins would it extinguish in the spark from which Christians have afterwards to be saved by being pulled out of the roaring fire? How often would it check a deviation at the beginning which ends in our going far astray, and losing a peace which in this world we may never fully recover? In how many cases would it, by early sending us to the balm of Gilead, heal wounds that, neglected, fester into deep, running, sores? And as I have seen the workman, ere he retired to rest, throw himself into stream or sea to wash away the sweat and dust of his daily toil, from such a review the Christian would repair each evening to the fountain of Jesus' blood to be cleansed of the guilt of daily sins; and rise each morning to seek the aids of the Holy Spirit to do his work, to keep his watch, to bear his burden, to fight his battle, better. If balancing our accounts with God, if reviewing the day's transactions, showed no progress in the divine life, what earnestness and liveliness would it impart to our evening prayers? If, on the contrary, it showed some good done, some sin crucified, some progress made, what a comfort, as we laid our head on the pillow, to think that we were nearer heaven than when we first believed, and that, with Jesus standing by the helm, our bark, whether gliding smoothly over calm or tossed in tempestuous seas, was approaching the shores of the happy land—the home and haven of our eternal rest!

IX.

The Parable of the Lost Piece of Money.

Luke xv. 8—10.

It is a grand sight, lion-hunters tell us, to see the forest-king at bay. Driven from his bloody lair, and pursued by men and dogs till further flight is useless, he turns round to face his foes; and when he confronts them,—lashing his sides with his tail, his shaggy mane bristling all erect, fire flashing from his terrible eyes, and thunder roaring from his throat,—the coward crowd fall back; there is death in the spring for which he is bending, and only the bravest stand. Here the Lion of the tribe of Judah is brought to bay. Jesus stands face to face with his enemies; but how different the spectacle, and the passions which it expresses! For the purpose of blackening his reputation, the Scribes and Pharisees, his malignant and implacable foes, resort to the basest insinuations; and the Son of God has to stand on his defence. He might have said, and with more reason than Jonah, "I do well to be angry," and, turning with indignation on His accusers, covered these whited sepulchres with confusion and with shame. But how meek and gentle his bearing, and how triumphant his defence! When one reads in these beautiful stories of the poor wandering sheep, of the lost money, and of the erring but repentant and forgiven prodigal, how does this apology, this justification of himself for associating with sinners, recall to our recollection the words,—

> "Not to condemn the sons of men,
> The Son of God appeared;
> No weapons in His hand are seen,
> Nor voice of terror heard!"

When suffering from calumny, it is usually the wisest plan to follow John Wesley's practice, and, without reply from either tongue or pen, to let our life refute it, as he said, "to live it down." The lie, the foul and false insinuation, which bad men use to destroy the reputation of the good, is like mud. While it is wet, it sticks; but, since to attempt to wash it out often only spreads the stain, it is best to leave it alone; and drying, in a short while it falls off of itself. It is not uncommon for those who cannot refute, to revile; but a man who has confidence in the goodness of his cause, and walking in his integrity, is conscious of the purity of his motives, is a polished mirror, from whose face, though awhile obscured, the breath of scandal shall vanish, nor leave a stain behind.

When the interests of a great cause, however, are at stake, and attempts are made to stab it through the sides of its advocate, to destroy it by destroying his reputation, he may find it necessary, much as he might prefer quietly to bear wrong, to act in self-defence.

Such, in his judgment, appear to have been the circumstances in which our Lord was placed. His enemies, for the purpose of bringing discredit on his cause, had attempted to injure his character; and that by the most insidious of all ways; by insinuation, more than by a bold and open attack. "This man," said they, "receiveth sinners, and eateth with them." Looking at that remark in the light of the adage, "Tell me your company, and I will tell you your character," it is easy to see what they meant. It was saying, in other words, He keeps low company; if like draws to like, and birds of a feather flock together, this Jesus is no better than he should be; if he were a man of pure mind and virtuous life, would he accept invitations to the tables of people of infamous character?—would he outrage public decency and obliterate the difference between good and bad men, virtue and vice, by eating and drinking with publicans and sinners? I can fancy them using even Scripture to feather the poisoned arrow; and, as they pointed to Jesus breathing words of hope into the ear of some poor fallen woman, or kindly trying to raise a publican from his degradation, I can imagine them asking, with the sneer of a fiend and the tongue of a serpent, Can that be David's son?—the son of him who said, Blessed is the man that standeth not in the way of sinners! I am a companion of all them that fear Thee. I have not sat with vain persons, neither will I go in with dissemblers; I have hated the congregation of evil-doers, and will not sit with the wicked?

It was the purest love which drew our Lord to sinners. He was among them, but holy, harmless, and undefiled—separate, as oil among the water it swims in, or as the sunbeam which, lighting up the dun and dusty air, passes through it without contracting the slightest stain. Yet with such vile aspersions was Jesus rewarded for leaving the bosom of his Father, and the society of angels, to save the lost! A physician, suddenly summoned to the bed of poverty and disease, leaves his home to face the pelting, midnight storm, and spend the hours others give to rest endeavoring, with all tenderness and highest skill, to alleviate the agony and save the life of some miserable wretch who, as she quaffed the cup of vice, has reached its lowest, bitterest dregs; and foul-tongued slanderers take occasion, from this act of pure, self-denying, and unrewarded benevolence, to cast reflections on his habits or his heart. Though nothing is more painful than to have kind and good and noble and generous actions imputed to the basest motives, yet the followers of Christ need not wonder, or be deterred from doing good by having that wrong to suffer. As this case shows, their Lord himself was not exempt from it. He was tried in all points like as we are; and when his people find, by a similar experience, that the servant is no better off than his Master, nor the disciple than his Lord, would God they were able to copy his pattern —to copy it as faithfully as a warrior did on a late battle-field! Riding over the ground when the fight was done, he came, as he picked his steps among the dead, to a body which, stirring, showed some signs of life. The bleeding form wore the dress of a foe. Regardless of that, he said to his attendant, "Give him a draught of wine;" and, as the officer stooped down to do so, the wounded soldier, discovering, through the mists that were gathering on his dying eye, in this good Samaritan the general of the troops against which he had been fighting, raised himself on his elbow, drew a pistol, and with deadly hate, fired it at his benefactor's head. Happily, the bullet missed its mark; and the general, so soon as he recovered from his surprise, with a forgiveness truly magnanimous said, "Give it him all the same!" But the attack made on our Lord's character under cover of the remark, This man receiveth sinners, did more than present Him with an opportunity of patiently bearing wrong, and generously forgiving the wrong-doer. Though we have not to thank his enemies for the vile aspersion, we have to thank God that he permitted it. In the words of Joseph, God meant it unto good. To this attack we owe our Lord's noble and unanswerable defence,—those three beautiful and blessed parables which, explaining why he did not shun but rather sought the company of sinners, have kindled hope in the bosom of despair, and encouraged thousands, like the poor prodigal, to return to their Father's house and cast themselves on his boundless mercy. To crush some plants, is to bring out their poisonous juices and their offensive odors; but Jesus—and, to some extent, all true Christians resemble him—resembled the sweetbrier and rosemary, the lowly thyme and the evergreen myrtle, which smell the sweetest when they are hardest crushed,—bathing with fragrance the hands that bruise them.

Before directing our attention specially to the parable before us, and the woman who, with lighted candle and broom in hand, is sweeping her dusty floor, I may remark—

First, that all these three parables are told for the same purpose; and that, though to cursory readers they may appear the same in their matter as in their object, they are not so. They are not, like the reverberations of thunder, mere echoes of one peal; nor, in following up the first parable with the second and the second with the third, is our Lord, to borrow a figure from his old trade, like a carpenter who seeks by repeated blows of the same hammer to drive a nail in to the head. These parables were all told to show why Christ sought sinners, and to encourage sinners to seek Him. But there are sinners of different shades of character; and these, that none might despair, are described under three different figures:—that stupid, senseless wanderer, the lost sheep; that piece of money which, devoid of sensibility and unconscious of its fall, lies in the dust, and feels no desire whatever to be otherwise; and that wretched prodigal—born in happy circumstances, well and kindly and piously reared—who acts from his own bad will, with wicked determination resists a father's authority, and, sinning against light and conscience, leaves home to plunge overhead into the foulest depths of vice.

Secondly, I remark, in regard to these parables, that by itself none of the three gives a complete picture of the method of salvation. To see God aright as saving man, and man as saved by God, we must, if I may say so, dovetail them into each other, and make one picture of the three. For example, beautiful, touching, and instructive as is the story of the prodigal, still it gives no adequate idea of the part which God acts in our salvation. No doubt the father, so soon as he catches sight of the penitent yet a great way off, runs to meet him, and, ere the words of confession have left his lips, folds him to his bosom in the embraces of a free, full, flowing, overflowing forgiveness. But he does not send for him. No kind letters full of tender entreaties, no servant from the father's house, ever reaches the miserable swineherd; far less are the household amazed to see the father himself, or by his other and elder son, go forth, leaving home and its pleasures all behind, to seek the poor prodigal in the far country to which his steps have carried him, and amid the misery in which his sins have plunged him. There is an elder brother here; but how unlike ours! Careless of a brother's fate, he stays at home at ease; nor thinks of seeking him whose infant steps he had guided, and with whom, when the day's play was over, he had slept on one couch, the arms of the two boys entwined around each other's necks. He neither regrets his absence, nor rejoices at his return. Selfish and sulky, angry and jealous, that elder brother is a foil to ours. Instructive picture as this is of a sinner's misery and a penitent's heart, and of the joyous welcome given to the worst who repent and return, it is the other parables more than this that present a picture of God,—how he feels toward sinners, and what he does to save them. In these we see God seeking our salvation; not waiting till we go to him, but coming to us—to seek and to save the lost. The heart of man beats in the story of the prodigal; but in this the heart of God. There we see man saved; here we see God saving. Such is the meaning of the parable, where a woman, having ten pieces of silver and losing one of them, lights a candle, sweeps the house, and seeks diligently till she find it.

WHAT BEFELL THIS WOMAN?

She had ten pieces of silver, and of these she lost one. But one out of the ten coins was lost; but one out of the hundred sheep went astray; but one member of the "certain man's" family became a prodigal; although the numbers of those not lost in these parables differ, only *one* in each case was lost. Are we to infer from that circumstance, that ours is the only world which has been cursed by sin? We are certain that there are many worlds besides our own; and that—with all the twinkling stars we see, and millions we do not see, suns around which there probably roll worlds corresponding to the planets of our solar system—this earth bears no more proportion to creation than one quivering leaf to the foliage of a giant tree, it may be to all the leaves of a boundless forest; than a single grain of sand to all the sands that form the shores or strew the bed of ocean. Why should not we hope that Satan has never winged his way to those bright realms, nor set foot on them; and that, like the one lost sheep of the flock, the one lost piece of money, the one prodigal of the family, ours is the only world that, leaving its orbit, has wandered into darkness and away from God? It adds much to the glory of the starry firmament, to look up and believe that those spheres are the abodes of innocence;—not prisons of suffering, but palaces of pure delights, with virtues brilliant as their light, and inhabitants, whatever be their form, as loyal to their God as are the worlds they inhabit to the suns round which they roll; and that, had we ears as we have eyes to reach them, from those beautiful stars we should hear as they rolled nightly over us, when the lark has dropped into her dewy nest and the busy city has sunk to slumber, and the din of the world is hushed, voices in the sky, such as John heard like the sound of many waters, or the shepherds when they listened to the angels singing.

But, whoever may be meant by the nine pieces of silver which were not lost, it is man's soul which is certainly meant by the one which was; nor, in some respects, could any figure so well express our naturally depraved, degraded, and undone condition. We were not always, not once, not at first, what we are now. On its issue from the mint, this foul, defaced, dusty, and dishonored coin was bright; stamped with the image and superscription of a king. Even so man was originally made in the likeness of God: on the pure, untarnished metal of his soul God impressed his own holy image. And still in reason, in conscience, in a sense of right and wrong, in noble aspirations after immortality and in many things else which distinguish him from the brutes that perish, there remain such traces of his original state as we see of its ancient glory in the hoary battlements of an old ruin; or, according to the figure of this parable, as we see in a foul, worn, rusted coin, with here a letter, and there a mutilated feature of its original image and superscription. But sin, deforming man's soul more than death his body, has defaced this likeness, and, till God seeks and his Spirit renews us, has left us buried amid the foulness and dust of corruption; so that one might fancy that it was over not Abraham's, but all Adam's race, the bearded prophet stood, and raised, as he contemplated their miserable ruin, this lamentable cry, "How is the gold become dim! how is the most fine gold changed! the stones of the sanctuary are poured out in the top of every street. The precious sons of Zion, comparable to fine gold, how are they esteemed as earthen pitchers, the work of the hands of the potter!"

Not only this parable but all Scripture represents us as lost. Yet there is hope in the very circumstances in which we are lost. The case is bad, but not so bad as we can imagine it to have been. It is unfortunate to lose a piece of money in the house, but much more so in a field, or on a moor. Lost in the mountain fills a mother with alarm for her child; but lost at sea strikes her down with despair. Be it money or a living man, whatever, falling overboard and disappearing beneath the wave, is borne by its weight down and down to the bottom of the deep, is certainly, for ever, lost; and therefore God employs this figure to set forth his full and everlasting forgiveness of his people's sins. Enraptured with the thought, "Who," exclaims Micah, "is a God like unto thee, that pardoneth iniquity and passeth by the transgression of the remnant of his heritage? He retaineth not his anger forever, because he delighteth in mercy. He will turn again; he will have compassion upon us; he will subdue our iniquities: and thou wilt cast all their sins into the depths of the sea." Sins forgiven are lost in the sea; but souls under condemnation of the law and in danger of hell, are lost in the house. Though deformed by sin and defiled by corruption, yet, being within the house, thank God, they are within the region of hope and the reach of mercy. And with infinite love in Jesus Christ, and infinite mercy in the bosom of God, and infinite grace in the Holy Spirit, I despair of none being redeemed, any more than of the coin being recovered, though it had rolled into the darkest nook of the house, now that the woman has lighted her candle and swept the floor and cleared out every corner with her broom, and, stooping down, is turning the dust-heap over and over—seeking till the lost be found. So Jesus came, and so he comes, to seek and to save the lost.

WHAT THIS WOMAN DID TO FIND THE MONEY.

She did everything proper in the circumstances. Indeed she could not do more than she did,—image, though faint, of that work, the wonder of astonished heavens and the highest subject of angels' praise, of which, pointing to his Son, the bleeding victim of the accursed tree, God asks, "What could have been done more for my vineyard, that I have not done in it?" In regard to the steps which she took, we are, in judging of their propriety and necessity, to remember that Eastern houses are not constructed on the style of ours —pierced as they are with many windows to admit the welcome sunlight. In climates where comfort lies rather in excluding than admitting the rays of a burning sun, the houses are built of dead walls; and the rooms in consequence are dark even in the daytime. Therefore this woman lights a candle to see with, and search the house. In point of condition as well as construction, houses in the East differ from ours. The habits of the people are not cleanly; and the floors, being formed of dried mud, are dusty as well as the rooms dark; the fitter emblem such houses of our natural state—a darkened head and a polluted heart. Besides lighting a candle, therefore, the woman seizes a broom, and bending eager to her task, with candle lowered to the ground, she sweeps it; nor, breathing the choking air and moving in a cloud of dust, ceases till the coin, swept up, rings on the floor, or the light flashes on its silver edges; and gladly seizing it, she holds it aloft, and rushing out in the fulness of her joy, calls her neighbors to rejoice in her success.

We might like to know with certainty what character the woman here represents on the stage. But, though that point were as obscure as was her person amid the cloud of dust her broom had raised in the dark and dirty house, the candle shining in her hand

is undoubtedly the Bible, God's revealed Word. Assuming that she symbolizes the Spirit of God, it is when He takes that heavenly light, and, carrying it into the recesses of a man's soul, reveals its foulness and danger and misery, that the sinner discovers his loss; and, feeling his need of a Saviour, cries, What shall I do to be saved?—Create in me a clean heart, O God! As to the sweeping, which disturbs the house and reveals a foulness that so long as it lay unstirred was perhaps never suspected, that may indicate the convictions, the alarms, the dread discoveries, the searchings and agitations of heart, which not unfrequently accompany conversion. It is not till the glassy pool is stirred that the mud at the bottom rises to light; it is when storms sweep the sea that what it hides in its depths is thrown up on the shore; it is when brooms sweep walls and floor that the sunbeams, struggling through a cloud of dust, reveal the foulness of the house; and it is agitations and perturbations of the heart which reveal its corruption, and are preludes to the purity and peace that sooner or later follow on conversion. That money was not recovered without a great disturbance within the house; nor are souls, especially such as have been long and deeply sunk in sin, commonly converted without great trials, agitations, and searchings of heart. But, be their seat a diseased body or a troubled mind, how welcome should we make the sufferings which bring us to Christ, and end in our salvation—humbling us in the dust—weaning our affections from earth and wedding them to heaven!

This scene, though expressing the general truth that God has done everything to save lost souls which even He could do, conveys no idea whatever of the price of our salvation—at what an incalculable ransom we were redeemed. The curtain rises, and the stage shows us the interior of a house, and a woman, dimly seen through a cloud of dust, who is quietly, though carefully, sweeping the floor. There is no dying, no dreadful deed of violence, no mortal struggle, here; no blood bespatters the walls, or creeps in red stream over the floor; no passer-by starts and listens, and thinks he hears blows and groans issuing from within. There is nothing indicative of Christ having sacrificed his life for ours. The nature of the parable does not admit of it; yet we are never to forget that it was through suffering as well as seeking that we were saved; and that, to redeem us, God spared not even his own Son—commending his love to us in that, while we were sinners, Christ died for us.

THE WOMAN'S JOY AT FINDING THE PIECE OF SILVER.

There is a peculiar pleasure felt in recovering what we have lost; or in having anything placed beyond the reach of danger which we were afraid of losing. A group of children with health blooming on their rosy cheeks, joy ringing in their merry laughter, vigor bounding in their frames as they chase the butterfly or each other over the flowery lawn, is a sight to gladden any, but especially a parent's eye; yet it is a deeper joy to look on the pallid face and languid form of the child who, propped up on pillows and an object still of care and trouble never grudged, has been plucked from the jaws of death—brought back from the very gates of the grave. No boat making the harbor over a glassy sea, its snowy canvas filled by the gentle breeze and shining on the blue waters like a sea-bird's wing, is watched with such interest, or, as with sail flapping on the mast it grates on the shingle, is welcomed with such joy, as one which, leaving the wreck on the thundering reef, comes through the roaring tempest, boldly breasts the billows, and bringing off the half-drowned, half-dead survivors, shoots within the harbor amid flowing tears and cheers that, bursting from the happy crowd, rise above the rage and din of elements. No gathering of an unbroken, happy, prosperous family in their old home on the return of a birthday, or at Christmas time, ever filled a father's heart with such gratitude and gladness, as was felt in the house where, while the prodigal sat encircled by his father's arm, each happier than the other, the music that filled the air, the wine that flowed in bowls, the floor that shook to the dancers' feet, but feebly expressed the deep though silent joy which welled up in the old man's heart. By such scenes a gracious God, accommodating his language to our ideas, expresses his joy in saving sinners, and in seeing sinners saved. To entertain any other idea of him is to do injustice to his gracious character and to endanger our own souls. "As I live," saith the Lord, "I have no pleasure in the death of the wicked."—"What," he asks, "could have been done more for my vineyard, that I have not done in it?" To the edge of the grave, to the brink of perdition, I see him following the most obstinate and headstrong and perverse and wretched sinner, with this earnest and most affectionate entreaty, Turn ye, turn ye, why will ye die? Some wretched and heart-broken creature, the flower which has been trodden on the street where the villain hand that plucked had thrown it when its freshness and bloom were gone—one polluted in body and in mind—one lost to virtue and shunned by decency—one for whom none cared but a mother, who clung to hope, and with love burning in its ashes, wept and prayed in secret for her she never named, is converted; and think of God in heaven feeling more joy than the mother who on a wild winter's night has opened her door to the wanderer's moaning cry; and while she hastens to tell the glad tidings to humble and sympathizing neighbors, think of Him telling them to his angels, and calling them to rejoice with him that the dead is alive again and the lost is found; think of the joyful alacrity with which those happy, holy, spirits haste, if so employed, to do the Saviour's bidding—prepare another mansion and weave another crown.

What value belongs to these souls of ours, when the repentance and salvation even of one sinner is thought worthy of being published in heaven and sung to the music of angels' harps? We may be assured that it is from a dreadful doom the soul is saved; and that it was over a fearful abyss it hung when Jesus plucked it from the wreck. Angels had not otherwise turned an eager gaze from heaven on earth, and looked down from their lofty realms to watch the issue with breathless interest, and feel such joy at the result; and as I have seen a man when the wave, bearing the boat on its foaming crest, brought it up to the ship's side, seize the happy moment and with one great bound leap in, so should sinners, perilously hanging on the brink of ruin, over perdition, the hell that yawns below, seize the opportunity to be saved. Willing and eager to save, Christ stretches out his arms to receive us. Let us throw ourselves on his mercy, crying, Save now, Lord—Lord save me, I perish!

X.

The Parable of the Sower.

Matthew xiii. 3—23.

THE first snowdrop, the first green leaf on naked hedges, the first few notes that sounding from bush or tree break the long, dreary silence—still more the first smile that lights up an infant's face, its first gleam of intelligence, its first broken word, possess an interest and yield a pleasure peculiar to themselves. With more interest still—did the world hold such treasures —would we look on the first stanzas of Homer's muse; the first attempt of Archimedes' skill; the first oration of Demosthenes; the first sermon of Chrysostom; the first sketch of Rubens; though we could hope to see nothing in these but the dawn of talents, which, at maturity, produced their splendid works, and won them immortal fame. What gives the interest to these things, gives a peculiar interest to this parable. Others may be as instructive and as beautiful, but of all those parables that he strung like pearls on the thread of his discourses, this is the first Jesus ever spake. As peculiarly befitting him who came to sow saving truths broadcast on the world, no subject could form a more suitable introduction; and with the divine skill with which he chooses, Jesus handles the topic. For though his first, this parable bears no trace of the feebleness and imperfections that mark other, the greatest, men's earliest efforts—another illustration this of the words "He spake as never man spake," as with his foot on the waves, He walked as never man walked.

The circumstances in which our Lord was placed while—in addition to his look and voice—imparting to this discourse an impressiveness and liveliness which it loses within the dull walls either of church or room, very probably gave it its color and form. A crowd eager to catch every word that fell from his blessed lips, surging and pressing forward, besieged the house, where, now answering the cavils of the Pharisees, and now expounding the mysteries of the Gospel, he talked to the people. Kind and considerate, our Lord—since faith cometh by hearing, and hearing by the Word of God—that all might hear left the house; and, followed by a rushing, gathering throng, takes his way to the shores of the neighboring lake. There is room enough for all there. On reaching it he enters a boat, converting it into a pulpit; and when by a few strokes of the oars in John's or Peter's hands, the boat is shot a short way out, he turns to address the multitude who throng the shore—sitting or standing, tier above tier, on its shelving sides. Lighted by the sun, its roof heaven's own lofty dome, its walls the hills that girdled the lake, which, shining like a silver mirror, lay still and quiet at its Maker's feet, what edifice of man's ever offered preacher such a noble temple? The preacher was in keeping with the temple; no Barnabas, or Boanerges among the sons of the mighty to be likened to him who then and there, from the rude pulpit of a fishing-boat, consecrated shores, and fields, and hillsides for worship—teaching his servants to sow beside all waters, to be instant in season and out of season; and with all respect to the ordinary places and forms of divine service, to seize, without much regard either to time or place, every opportunity of preaching the blessed Gospel, and of saving them that are ready to perish. To fancy aright this scene, we must remember that the hills of Galilee, unlike those by some of our wild Highland lochs, do not descend right into the lake; nor, coming down steep and rocky, leave but a narrow footpath on the margin of the water. On the contrary, and especially on the western shores, between the feet of these hills and the lake, lies a broad belt of land, sloping gently down to the beach; and in our Lord's days, when the country teemed with inhabitants, and the shores all around were studded with towns and villages, this was cultivated by busy husbandmen, and rewarded their labor with abundant harvests. Now, it was on one of these fields which rose behind the throng, that our Lord's eye caught the object which suggested this parable. A man, very probably, like Martha, cumbered about many things, with a large family to support, with a heavy rent to meet, who thought he had no time, and perhaps had no inclination to drop work and join the crowd, comes forth from his house to sow. Jesus seizes the incident as the text for a sermon, a groundwork for instruction;

and waving his hand so as to turn the eyes of the assembly on the husbandman, He begins the parable, saying, "Behold, a sower went forth to sow."

This man, let it be observed, was not sowing a field like those around this city, where with hedge or wall the farmer fences his field from wandering feet; and by breaking up the rough parts of the ground, carefully weeding the foul, and feeding the bare and barren, gives a uniform aspect to the whole. Agriculture, stimulated by trade or the pressure of population on the means of subsistence, has made great progress since our Lord's days—rising from a comparatively rude art to the position of a science. And to enter fully into the scene of this parable and the meaning of its different parts, we must therefore leave these fat and fertile plains, to transport ourselves to those remote districts of the country where old customs linger, and the natural features of the landscape resemble those of the shores of Galilee. We find what we want in many of our Highland glens—the shores of their lakes presenting a counterpart of the field whose different features are woven into this parable. There, leading to a well, or to the nook where the boat lies moored, or to a neighbor's cottage, or to the parish church, we may see an old pathway skirting the borders of the field, or running right across it—in those places where the plough has rolled or rains have washed it down, the soil lies deep—elsewhere, on gravel or rocky knolls, it is poor and shallow—while here and there springing from cairns of stones, or parts imperfectly cleared and cultivated, whin and

broom, the wild rose, ferns, birches and dwarf-willows, lend a beauty to the field which is more picturesque than profitable. In the corresponding features of that field which lay in sight of his floating pulpit, Jesus saw striking emblems of the hearers of his own, and also of every other, congregation. As such he uses them; and bringing to his task the unrivaled skill which turned birds into teachers, drew the noblest truths out of the meanest subjects, and found in common things fresh texts for uncommon sermons, he reaped a harvest from this field other and better far than sickles had ever done. Its owner had never cultivated it to such purpose as the Great Husbandman. The preacher makes more of it than the plough; no part lies barren in Jesus' hands; no golden crops that bowed their heads to the winds which swept the lake of Galilee like the truths he drew from its different soils!—in solemn and salutary warnings, in the revelation of his work, of his character, and of his gospel, making it yield a perpetual harvest of the bread of life, for the use of his own and all future ages.

THE SOWER.

Sheltered from the winds that played on the breezy summits of the mountains, the lake of Galilee reflected the face and form of Jesus—his image was mirrored in its glassy depths. And such a mirror is this parable; presenting in the sower a true emblem and image of Christ himself. Of that there can be no doubt, though he does not say so in as many words; saying, in his explanation of the parable, I am the Sower, as, pointing on one occasion to a vine clasping in its arms a rock, which it clothed with broad leaves and hung with purple clusters, he said, I am the Vine; or on another occasion, pointing to the sun, as rolling out of the shadow of a cloud, or springing up from behind a hill, it bathed the whole landscape in golden glory, he said, I am the light of the world. With that kind and tender love which should touch and win our hearts, Jesus, leaving his Father's bosom, descended on our world not only to procure, but to preach salvation; with his own hand to sow, in the furrows that repentance had made, the seeds of eternal life. With this end in view he sent the Baptist to proclaim his advent, and prepare his way. In the order of things ploughing goes before sowing. The soil must be broken up, and, stirring it to its depths, the iron must enter its bosom, that verdure in summer may clothe, and tall sheaves in autumn crowd the field. Now, what the man with the plough is to his fellow who, with a sowing sheet around him, casts the grain into the open furrows, John Baptist, denouncing vice, unmasking hypocrites, sparing neither prince nor peasant, priests nor people, but calling all to repentance, was to Jesus Christ. He went sternly through the land, like an iron ploughshare,—breaking up the fallow ground, and preparing men to receive the tidings of salvation which Christ came to preach. Sovereigns do sometimes grant pardons; but, so far as I know, they never bring them. Little affected by the miseries of the wretch whose sighs and groans confined within stone walls never penetrate the palace to disturb the sleep or dash the pleasure of the court, kings content themselves with sending pardons through servants and cold officials; and such a thing as one leaving his palace, bending his steps to the prison, flying on wings of love, with his own lips to announce the tidings, and hear with his own ears, sound sweeter than finest music, the cry of joy from one plucked from the jaws of death, is untold in history. But Christ so loved us that he came himself with the good news. He who at a great price procured liberty to the captive also proclaimed it; and he who made this earth stood on it a preacher of salvation. No wonder Paul magnified his office, considering who had filled it; and no doubt it was the pleasure Jesus felt in the good news he preached which so glowed in his countenance, and lent such tenderness, and power, and pathos to his oratory, that a woman who heard him cried, Blessed is the womb that bare thee,—and his very enemies confessed, Never man spake like that man. Thus he sowed. Would that all his servants caught his spirit, and came to the pulpit wearing his mantle!

They are sowers also. Every preacher of the Gospel is a sower of the seed: and though the whole scene of this parable is now changed, and Galilee's lake lies among her silent hills, still a beautiful, but now a lonely sheet of water—though her shores are furrowed by no plough, and her sea by no fisherman's keel—though her cities live only in the pages of history, and have no place but on the geographer's map —though the traveler finds little there to remind him of Jesus but the waves that sustained his form, and the storms that as they sweep and vex the lake recall the memorable night when, waked from deep and dreamless slumbers, he rose to bid winds and waves be still—though eighteen hundred long years are gone, still I may make use of the words with which Jesus began his first public discourse, when, having read a passage from Isaiah, he closed the book and lifted up his head to say, This day is this Scripture fulfilled in your ears. When bells have rung out and the congregation, whether coming from hamlets and farms along sweet country roads, or from their houses through dry and dusty streets, are assembled, and as they wait in silence, a man enters the pulpit in robe of office or in ordinary attire, it may be said, as truly as on the day when Christ was the preacher and a boat the pulpit, Behold, a sower went forth to sow. It is the same seed we sow; and, in their hearts, congregations still present the same varieties of soil; but what a difference between this sower and his successors; his skill and our rudeness; his power and our weakness; his love and our cold affections; his burning zeal and our feeble fires; the light of the world and the flame of a taper —ay, the brightest star that ever shone in the firmament of the Church! Well may we say with Paul, "Brethren, pray for us!"

> "Except the Lord do build the house
> The builders lose their pain,
> Except the Lord the city keep
> The watchmen watch in vain."

The Spirit in Christ's day, not yet given in showers, or otherwise than in scattered drops, even he himself sowed to little purpose; a few hundred converts the whole result of his labors, and of such labors, how little the joy, how scant the harvest? What, then, can sustain the preacher in his study or his pulpit, but faith in the promises, in God's own word that, by his own Spirit, he will with the foolish things of the world so confound the wise, and with the weak things of the world so confound the things that are mighty, that "he who goeth forth and weepeth, bearing precious seed, shall doubtless come again with rejoicing, bringing his sheaves with him."

THE SEED.

This, as Christ explains, is "the word of the Kingdom,"—those saving, Bible truths of which Paul speaks, saying, Woe be unto me if I preach not the Gospel. His kingdom, it is "*the* kingdom" by way of excellence, there being no other of which, having seen the rise, it shall not see also the fall—*the* kingdom, in contradistinction to those which, rivers, shores, or mountains bound—many of which founded in injustice, and maintained by oppression, have tyrants for their rulers, and for their subjects slaves; and all of which, if I may judge the future by the past, have this course to run—born, they grow, arrive at maturity, flourish for a longer or shorter period, then begin to decay; and, sinking under the infirmities of age, or falling by the hands of violence, at length expire—their palaces a heap of ruins, their kings a handful of dust.

As different from these in its character as in its

duration, the kingdom here is that over which Jesus reigns—justice his law, love his rule, mercy his sceptre, peace his government, and the only weapon he employs to conquer his enemies and govern his subjects, the Bible. By that he rules; on that his kingdom rests—God's inspired Word, true without any mixture of error, and suffering as little from the assaults of sceptics, secret or avowed, as yon castle rock from the storms which, raving and howling around its solid crags, have blown, but not blown it away.

In regard to the figure here. None—not leaven with its assimilating power, nor light with its illuminating rays, nor bread with its nutritious elements, nor water as it springs sparkling from a mossy fountain to parched and thirsty lips—none sets forth the word of God better than this of seed. For example:—

There is life in Seed.—Dry and dead as it seems, let a seed be planted with a stone-flashing diamond, or burning ruby; and while that in the richest soil remains a stone, this awakes and, bursting its husky shell, rises from the ground to adorn the earth with beauty, perfume the air with fragrance, or enrich men with its fruit. Such life there is in all, but especially in Gospel, truth. It lives when we die—as the old martyr exclaimed, when he stood bound to the fiery stake, Me you may kill; the truth you cannot! This is the incorruptible and immortal seed; and though ornaments, polish, illustrations, eloquence in sermons may help the end in view, as feathers do the arrow's flight, or their wings the thistle-downs, as they float, sailing through the air, to distant fields, it is to the truth of God's Word, blessed by God's Spirit, that sinners owe their conversion, and saints their quickening and comfort in the house of God. The patient is healed by the medicine, not by what gilds it: the hungry are fed by the meat, not by what garnishes it; these fields crowded with joyous reapers and covered with golden sheaves show the life that was in the seed, not in the sower, or in the soil; and conversions being due not to the human talent but to the divine truths in the sermon, the greatest as well as the feeblest preachers have to say, Not unto us, not unto us; but unto thee, O Lord, be all the glory!

There is force in Seed.—Buried in the ground a seed does not remain inert,—lie there in a living tomb. It forces its way upward, and with a power quite remarkable in a soft, green, feeble blade, pushes aside the dull clods that cover it. Wafted by winds or dropped by passing bird into the fissure of a crag, from weak beginnings the acorn grows into an oak—growing till by the forth-putting of a silent but continuous force, it heaves the stony table from its bed, rending the rock in pieces. But what so worthy to be called the power as well as the wisdom of God as that Word which, lodged in the mind, and accompanied by the divine blessing, fed by showers from heaven, rends hearts, harder than the rocks, in pieces? "He that hath my word," says God, "let him speak my word faithfully. What is the chaff to the wheat, saith the Lord? Is not my word like as a fire, and like a hammer that breaketh the rock in pieces?"

There is a power of propagation in Seed.—Thus a single grain of corn would, were the produce of each season sown again, so spread from field to field, from country to country, from continent to continent, as in the course of a few years to cover the whole surface of the earth with one wide harvest,—employing all the sickles, filling all the barns, and feeding all the mouths in the world. Such an event, indeed, could not happen in nature, because each latitude has its own productions, and there is no plant formed to grow alike under the sun of Africa, and amid the snows of Greenland. It is the glory of the Gospel, and one of the evidences of its divine origin-that it can: and, unless prophecy fail, that it shall. There is not a shore which shall not be sown with this seed; not a land but shall yield harvests of glory to God and of souls for heaven. By revolutions that are overturning all things, by war's rude and bloody share, and otherwise, God is breaking up the fallow ground, and ploughing the earth for a glorious seed-time. The seed that sprang up in Bethlehem shall wave over arctic snows and desert sands: and as every shore is washed by one sea, and every land that lies between the poles is girdled by one atmosphere, and every drop of blood that flows in human veins belongs to one great family of brothers, so in God's set time men of every color and tongue shall cherish a common faith, and trust in a common Saviour. It was of that, and of this seed-time, the Psalmist spoke, when standing on the heights of prophecy, and looking along the vista of distant ages, he said, "There shall be a handful of corn in the earth on the top of the mountains; the fruit thereof shall shake like Lebanon." "His name,"—referring to Christ—"His name shall endure forever; men shall be blessed in him, and all nations shall call him blessed." Thus the seer spake; and while we echo his devout "Amen and Amen," let us pray, Even so come, Lord Jesus, come quickly!

THE SOIL.

Hearers represented by the Wayside.—"When he sowed, some seeds fell by the wayside, and the fowls came and devoured them up." Nothing more likely to happen! No care, with broad cast sowing, could prevent some seed falling on the pathway where, as that was beaten hard by the feet of passengers, it lay exposed to birds which, as all know, in spring, ere buds have burst, or sunny skies tempted insects forth, or genial showers called worms from their holes, often suffer from want of food. Made bold by hunger, our birds, some from the woods sailing on raven's wing, others with snowy plumage from neighboring shores, attend the ploughman as he turns up the furrows and their food; so yonder in the fields of Galilee they watch the motions of the husbandman, and sweep down from rock or tree to pick up the grains that lie on the beaten road.

The explanation of this scene Jesus gives in these words: "When any one heareth the word of the kingdom, and understandeth it not, then cometh the wicked one, and catcheth away that which was sown in his heart: this is he which received seed by the wayside"

—Mark says, "Satan cometh immediately, and taketh away the word"—Luke says, "Then cometh the devil, and taketh away the word out of their hearts, lest they should believe and be saved." Again I say, nothing more likely to happen. Some who carefully cultivate their fields, or their gardens, or their business, or their minds, take no pains whatever to cultivate their hearts. The Bible neglected, prayer, unless as a mere form, a plough passed over the surface, unused, no serious thought given from week's end to week's end to another world and their precious souls, their hearts are like ground ploughshare has never entered. Worse still, in a worse state than an uncultivated waste, the world with its many, hurrying, heavy feet has been trampling over their poor hearts the whole week through—day by day, year by year, from early childhood, perhaps, to gray old age; till under the ceaseless tread and tramp and traffic of worldly thoughts, unholy desires, selfish and evil passions, they have grown harder with time, and become as unimpressible and impenetrable almost as a stone. They are without God in the world. He is in the sky above and in the earth beneath them, in the air they inhale and in the bread they eat, by their side when they walk and by their bed when they sleep, everywhere but where most of all he should be: he is not in all their thoughts; and bringing to his house hearts as hard as the flags they walk on, no wonder that their hearing and our preaching is vain!

The case as painted in this parable, and in truth, —for this is no fiction,—is worse still. So bad, indeed, that but for the mercy that pities the poorest sinners, and the might that can turn a heart of stone into one of flesh, we could cherish no hope of doing them any good. Wherever there is a preacher in the pulpit, there is a devil among the pews, busy, watching the words that fall from the speaker's lips to catch them away, and, by the idle, worldly, evil thoughts—the birds that pick up the seed—which he intrudes on them, to prevent the word making an impression or remove any it happens to make. What an illustration of this the speech which a dying, despairing man addressed to one under whose ministry he had sat for twenty years! I have never, he cried, heard a single sermon! The minister, to whom his face was quite familiar, who had known him for years as a regular attender at church, looked astonished—fancied that he was raving under the delirium of his approaching end. No, not at all! The man was in his sad and sober senses. I attended church, he explained, but my habit was, so soon as you began the sermon, to begin a review of last week's trade, and to anticipate and arrange the business of the next. Now, in like manner, to a greater or less extent, Satan deals with thousands who occupy pews in the church. Doing so, distracting their attention, playing with their fancy, carrying away their minds to outside scenes of business or pleasure, "lest they should believe and be saved." Thus he destroys souls, not in his own devilish haunts, but in the very house of God; wrecking them at the very mouth of the harbor; slaying them on the very steps of the altar; turning their attendance on ordinances into a means of hardening their hearts and aggravating their final, dreadful doom, he, if I may say so, seethes the kid in its mother's milk. Since Christ's own presence did not scare the fiend from the room where the disciples had met for the Church's greatest and most solemn rite; since, stealing into the chamber, he entered into Judas when his hand was dipped into the same dish with Christ's, how should we watch, keep our hearts and keep our feet when we enter the house of God,—in the words of Peter, Be sober, be vigilant, because our adversary, the Devil, as a roaring lion, walketh about seeking whom he may devour.

Hearers represented by the Stony Ground.—In Spring, before the growth hides the ground, I have seen fields sown out with corn so thick of stones that they seemed the substitutes for soil. I have heard people wonder what could induce any man in his senses to cultivate such land; yet they would wonder more to see the crops such soil, where the roots wind round the stones and bore away down in search of food, yields to the reaper's sickle. It is not such ground, though misunderstanding the term *stony ground* some may suppose so, which is described here; but that which, while the other parts of the field are green and healthy is marked in summer by a yellow, sickly hue. There the soil lies shallow—spread like a skin on bones of rock: and so, though a braird soon appears with fair and early promise of an abundant crop, the plants, having no depth of earth, are scorched by the sun; and, drawing no nourishment from the rock which their roots embrace, soon wither away.

In explanation of this part of the parable, our Lord says, "He that received the seed into stony places, the same is he that heareth the word, and anon with joy receiveth it; yet hath he not root in himself, but dureth for a while; for when tribulation or persecution ariseth because of the word, by and by he is offended," or, as it is given by Luke, "They on the rock are they, which, when they hear, receive the word with joy; and these have no root, which for a while believe, and in time of temptation fall away." These are alarming words. The matter is more serious than it was, since other than wayside hearers miss heaven. What have we here? the word listened to with attention; with more, much more than attention; with such feelings as a man under sentence of death hears the news of his pardon, or men on a wreck, lashed to the mast, hanging on the shrouds, hear the cry, the joyful cry, A boat! a life boat! People count on heaven to whom the Sabbath is a weariness, and a sermon dulness; yet here are those who, though they receive the word, according to one Evangelist, with "joy," and according to another with "gladness," come short of eternal life. Nor is the impression the truth produces a mere feeling, a passing emotion; vanishing with the tears it brings to their eyes; going down like the sea-swell when winds are hushed; dying away like some sweet strain of music when the hand is removed that struck the trembling strings. On the contrary the impression passes out into expression; they move out of the passive into the active state—making a good profession, and entering on the practice of religion. More, and more marked still, as the braird on shallow ground rises sooner than that which springs from deeper soil, the conversion (as it is supposed to be) of stony ground hearers is often marked by precocious piety, and a forward, flaming zeal. I have known most melancholy instances of that; and in all such cases, as some have fearfully illustrated, the last state of such persons is worse than the first. Let all of us take warning; let each prove his own work—whether he has in true, saving faith what is the root of the matter.

Paul had such hearers, whom he addresses, saying, "Ye did run well, what did hinder you?" John Baptist had many such, and in Herod a distinguished one—the only king, so far as I know, who felt such interest in religion as to break through established routine and leave his court chaplain to listen to a street preacher. His conduct in this matter, the pleasure he felt in the ministry of the fearless and faithful Baptist, the many things he did at John's bidding and advice, were full of promise—never soil was covered with a greener braird—never sky was lighted with a brighter dawn. He dured for a while; then fell away—and what a fall!—quenching the hopes, which God's people had begun to cherish of a pious king, in the blood of the martyred, murdered preacher. Not Paul, or the Baptist only, but our Lord himself had many such hearers. Crowds followed him; tracked his steps from city to city, from shore to shore—hanging on his lips, thronging the streets through which he passed, and besieging the houses where he lodged. The day was once when ten thousand tongues would have spoken and ten thousand swords would have flashed in his defence; and the day arrived when, during for a while, they fell away, and of the crowds that swelled his jubilant train, all, all deserted him—the only voice lifted up in his behalf coming from the cross of a dying thief.

The explanation of these, and of all cases where religion disappears and dies out under the influence either of temptation or of persecution, lies here—they had no root, no true faith. Convictions were mistaken for conversion; admiration of the servant for attachment to his master; an appreciation of the moral beauties of the gospel for an appreciation of its holiness; the pleasures of emotion, or such gratification as taste enjoys in a beautiful discourse, for the pleasures of piety. Beneath such promising appearances there lies a stony heart; and so when the tests of suffering or of temptation are applied, they fall away, like the multitude who, offended at Jesus' saying, walked no more with him.

Where however there is true faith, his people, thank God, need not much dread such trials. Resting firmly on the Rock of Ages, they are as Mount Zion which cannot be moved. To borrow the figure here, the hotter the sun, if the heavens send it showers, and the earth give it soil, the plant grows the taller and the stronger—grace growing in converted hearts like corn in strong, deep, rich, well watered soils. The warmer the summer, the richer the harvest.

Those represented by the Ground with Thorns.—Of the seed our Lord says "Some fell among thorns, and the thorns sprang up and choked them;" explaining it thus, "He also that receiveth seed among the thorns is he that heareth the word, and the care of this world, and the deceitfulness of riches, and," as Mark adds, "the lusts of other things entering in, choke the word, and it becometh unfruitful."

The regions which lie mid-way between the equator and the poles are proved by experience to be most favorable to life and its enjoyments; and so those conditions which lie mid-way between the opposite extremes of poverty and riches, are found most conducive to man's spiritual welfare. The proof of that which this parable, as well as many other passages of Scripture, presents, should warn both rich and poor of their peculiar dangers; and teach contentment to such of us as are fortunate enough to be neither harassed with the cares of poverty, nor tempted by the deceitfulness of riches. The danger and deceitful influence of riches, their tendency to turn our thoughts away from another world, and drown such concern for the soul as providences or preachers may have awakened, in the cup of pleasure, is awfully expressed in the saying of our Lord, "It is easier for a camel to go through the eye of a needle, than for a rich man to enter into the kingdom of God." Dr. Johnson put the point well when, on Garrick showing him his beautiful mansion and grounds, the great moralist and good man laid his hand kindly on the player's shoulder, and said, "Ah! David, David, these are the things which make a death-bed terrible!"

The equally dangerous and deadly influence of

great poverty I may illustrate by a scene which I have not forgotten, nor can forget. Alone, in the garret of a dilapidated house, within a wretched room, stretched on a pallet of straw, covered only by some scanty, filthy rags, with no fire in the empty chimney, and the winter wind blowing in cold and fitful gusts through the broken, battered window, an old woman lay, feeble, wasted, gray. She had passed the eleventh hour; the hand was creeping on to the twelfth. Had she been called? It was important to turn to the best account the few remaining sands of life; so I spoke to her of her soul, told her of a Saviour—urging her to prepare for that other world on whose awful border her spirit was hovering. She looked; she stared; and raising herself on her elbow, with chattering teeth, and ravenous look, muttered "I am cold and hungry." Promising help, I at the same time warned her that there was something worse than cold and hunger. Whereupon, stretching out a naked and skinny arm, with an answer which if it did not satisfy the reason touched the feelings, she said, "If you were as cold and as hungry as I am you could think of nothing else." The cares of the world were choking the word.

And so may, what Mark calls, "the lusts of other things" do—in such as are placed in the happy medium between wealth and want, strangling good thoughts in their very birth: destroying the fairest promises of conversion. Let me illustrate this also by an example. Robert Burns, who had times of serious reflection, in one of which, as recorded by his own pen, he beautifully compares himself, in the review of his past life, to a lonely man walking amid the ruins of a noble temple, where pillars stand dismantled of their capitals, and elaborate works of purest marble lie on the ground, overgrown by tall, foul, rank weeds—was once brought, as I have heard, under deep convictions. He was in great alarm. The seed of the word had begun to grow. He sought counsel from one called a minister of the Gospel. Alas, that in that crisis of his history he should have trusted the helm to the hands of such a pilot! This so-called minister laughed at the poet's fears—bade him dance them away at balls, drown them in bowls of wine, fly from these phantoms to the arms of pleasure. Fatal, too pleasant advice! He followed it: and "the lusts of other things" entering in, choked the word.

Now, be it woman's household cares or the anxieties and annoyances of man's business, the harassments of poverty or the enticements of wealth, the pursuit of fame or power, or pleasure, whatever in short it be that engrosses our attention, and, stealing our thoughts from God, and our hearts from heaven, counteracts the holy influences of Bibles, churches, sermons, Sabbaths, it is choking the word. We need to be on our guard. It is not the green and tender corn only which is smothered. I have seen the stately tree, with roots struck deep in the soil, and giant arms that had battled with the tempest, fall a prey to a low and ignoble creeper; fastening on it, rising on it, twining its pliant branches around the massive trunk, binding it more and more closely in its fatal embraces, the weak strangled the strong—to death. What but God's great grace and mercy, the timely interposition of Heaven, in his peril and extremity saved King David from becoming a ruin, a wreck as great as Demas the apostate, or Judas the traitor? The devil's hand was fastened on his throat, when Nathan appeared to loose it. Watch, therefore, and pray, that ye enter not into temptation—Let him that thinketh he standeth take heed lest he fall.

Those represented by the Good Ground.—"He," says our Lord, "that received seed into the good ground is he that heareth the word and understandeth [Mark says "receiveth]" it: which also beareth fruit, and bringeth forth, in some an hundred fold, some sixty, some thirty;" or as it is given by Luke, "The good ground are they which in an honest and good heart, having heard the word, keep it, and bring forth fruit with patience." In these words we are presented with certain salient, distinctive points of character,—touchstones, by which each man may, and should, try himself. In doing little else than indicating these, I remark of true Christians,

First, *They receive the Word.* In their case it does not, so to speak, go in at the one ear, and come out at the other. It does not fall on their minds to run off like water from a stone; it falls, but it is as seed into a furrow, to lodge itself in their hearts. They do not reject, but receive it.

Secondly, *They understand it,*—appreciate its value; feel its power; and "comprehend with all saints what is the breadth, and length, and depth, and height of the love of Christ, which passeth knowledge." But "the darkness," as the apostle John says, "comprehendeth it not." Did others comprehend, understand the truth in the highest sense of the term, would they act as they do? No! no more than a man, even a child, who understood the nature of fire, would walk into the burning flames. Did yonder savage know, or even dream of, its value, would he give a handful of gold to purchase a few worthless beads, a looking-glass, some fragile, infant's toy? Still less would yonder sinner, did he rightly understand the meaning of God's wrath, of God's love, of the cross of Calvary, of eternity, pawn his soul and peril its salvation for pleasures which perish in the using.

Thirdly, *They keep the Word:* as—in contradistinction to soils that puffed up by winter frosts throw out, or others that starve, their plants—good ground keeps the corn. Esteemed a treasure more precious than gold, yea than much fine gold, they lay the word in their hearts, locking it up there.—Its effect on others is temporary, as truths written on sands within the tide-mark where waves roll in, nor leave a letter there. On them its effects are permanent, not passing; deep, not shallow; the work of God's Spirit, not of man's powers of persuasion; such as Job wished: "O that my words were written! O that they were printed in a book! that they were graven with an iron pen in the rock for ever!" With hearts where the tenderness of flesh is associated with the tenaciousness of stone, as granite keeps the letters of its inscription, so they "keep the Word."

Fourthly, *They bring forth Fruit.*—In the form of

good works, of unselfish, gentle, and heavenly dispositions, of useful, noble, holy, and Christian lives, they bring forth fruit—some much; some little; but all some. "Neither barren nor unfruitful in the knowledge of our Lord Jesus Christ," they prove their faith by their works. So living, within a wide or narrow circle, when they die they are missed: and their memory, while "the name of the wicked shall rot," embalmed in their virtues and long preserved from decay, remains fragrant—as withered rose-leaves in a vase of spices.

Such are some of the points which distinguish real Christians from those who, however fair, are mere professors. The key to all lies here—they have, what is meant by the "good ground," a good heart,—what Luke calls "an honest and good heart,"—in other words a true and a new heart. Implanted at conversion, entailed on no heir, the natural inheritance of no man, this heart is found in those only who, born again of the Holy Ghost, have received the truth in the love of it. Its presence or absence explains what is otherwise inexplicable—in the same family, some reprobate and others religious; among disciples of the same Master, a Judas and a John; hanging one on each side of the same cross, an impenitent and a penitent thief; leaving the same church after listening to the same sermon, one sinner converted and another hardened. How important,—the term is too feeble, —how indispensable, absolutely indispensable, would men be saved, nor go to hell with a Bible hung like a millstone round their neck, this new heart! God can give it. He has given it wherever it has been got. There is nothing in the grains of corn to change bad ground into good; but this seed has the wondrous power of changing the nature of the soil. Blessed of God, the truth sanctifies. What therefore though the heart by nature is like a stone? The finest soils of earth were once stone; and He who by the action of stormy waves and stupendous icebergs ground down the rocks which reared their naked, rugged heads above the waste of waters into soil where now the ploughman draws his furrows and flashing sickles reap their richest harvest, can work such changes on hearts of stone. And he will, if we ask him. "If a son," says our Lord, "shall ask bread of any of you that is a father, will he give him a stone? or if he ask a fish, will he for a fish give him a serpent? or if he shall ask an egg, will he offer him a scorpion? If ye then, being evil, know how to give good gifts unto your children, how much more shall your heavenly Father give the Holy Spirit to them that ask him?"

XI.

The Parable of the Unmerciful Servant.

Matthew xviii. 21—25.

THE boy who, catching a poor fluttering insect, impales it, and then with curious and eager eyes watches it spin round and round, may not be of a cruel disposition. It is right by instruction, or by the rod even, to teach children kindness to the meanest thing that lives, still this barbarous and apparently cruel act may be entirely due to ignorance. The child does not know the pain it inflicts; and may just illustrate in the nursery what is so often illustrated by older people in the world, how, in miseries unrelieved, feelings wounded, and the poor neglected, more ill is done for want of thought than for want of heart. The nursery however presents a scene where, as through a rent in that veil of innocence which throws its sweetest charms over infancy, we see the bad passions of our nature. Proud and pleased as it takes its first steps across the floor to the mother, kneeling with radiant smiles and open arms to receive it, the infant totters, and falls with a lurch against chair or table. In such a case it is easier to stanch its wound than calm its anger. And yet, though the remedy is worse than the disease, that may be done. Revenge, says one, is sweet. There is nothing smells so sweet, said Louis XII., as the dead body of an enemy; and blowing up a spark she should have quenched, the foolish nurse or mother pretends, by beating chair or table, to avenge the wrong. The device succeeds—though it be, after a fashion, casting out devils by Beelzebub the prince of devils, and by another voice than his who spake peace to the storm of Galilee, calming the passions of that little bosom. Alas, her success in soothing anger by gratifying the passion for revenge, proves not so much the nurse's skill, as that forgiveness is not a virtue that belongs to our fallen nature.

To say that we forgive, is easy. But when engaged as a peacemaker, how have I seen the manner give the lie to the speech, and in the clouded brow, and sullen look, and reluctant advance, and cold hand of this scene, the strongest contrast to that where his father, seeing the prodigal afar off, runs to meet him, and rushes into his arms to kiss him? It is the forgiveness of the heart which God links to the forgiveness of the heavens—that which recalls Calvary, with Jesus bending eyes of pity on his murderers,—not the death-bed of an old highland chief in the days when clans met clans in deadly feud. It is told that the minister urged him to make his peace with men as well as with God, declaring that he could not expect to be forgiven unless he forgave. The word at length passed his reluctant lips; but, as if that dying chamber had been a stage, and the dying man an actor, who, having played his part, doffs his theatrical attire to resume his real character, so soon as it was spoken, he turned on his son to say, that he left him a father's curse if he forgave them!

Foreign to nature, forgiveness is difficult even to grace,—so difficult, that he who suffers a wrong and feels no impulse to retaliate, recalls one without aught of malice, endures cruel wounds which heal without festering into corrupt, acrid humors, has, if such grace there be on earth, reached its highest pinnacle; and presents the finest image of Him, who, when reviled, reviled not again, and when his mangled form lay stretched on the cross, raised his meek eyes to pray, "Father, forgive them, for they know not what they do!" This grace, be it observed, is not incompatible with a deep sense of our wrongs. The apathy which feels a blow no more than a stone does, an insult no more than the cold corpse which, spit upon, lifts no hand to wipe off the stain, a wound no more than the air which the arrow cleaves, or the water which kisses the prow and closes its arms around the keel that tears its bosom, does not constitute a forgiving temper. They forgive most who feel the deepest indignation at ingratitude, and on whom injuries inflict the keenest pain. On them as, in forgiving wrong, and returning good for evil, achieving the greatest victory over self, the wise man pronounces his high eulogium, "He that ruleth his spirit is better than he that taketh a city."

So foreign is this grace to humanity, that we are unable not only to practise but even fully to understand it—as is shown by the question which formed the occasion of this parable. Although the law of vengeance, as expressed by the proverb, "an eye for an eye and a tooth for a tooth," was the rule in Heathendom, God's ancient people had some notion of the duty of forgiveness. The dyer's hands are stained by the colors of his trade, and the very clothes of one who works among spices steal some of their fragrant perfume: so their familiarity with those Scriptures where God's forgiveness is so eagerly sought and highly extolled, inspired the Jews, to some extent, with a forgiving spirit. They held forgiveness to be a duty, binding up to the third offence; but beyond that limit, let the wrongdoer beware; outside that charmed circle, man had a right to say, with God, Vengeance is mine, I will repay. Now, Simon Peter had not lived these months or years with Jesus without catching something of his Master's gentle, placable, forgiving spirit. The leaven had begun to work; and his heart, swelling with something of Jesus's love, found the narrow limits of Jewish forgiveness too contracted for it. Though imperfect as the vision of him who, with sight but partially restored, saw men as trees walking, he had caught a glimpse of the truth: and came to Jesus, saying, "Lord, how oft shall my brother sin against me, and I forgive him? Seven times?" Hail to the dawn! The night is past, and the sky shows the first bright streaks of morning. "Seven times?" Simon has stept out in advance of the men of his age and nation; and our Lord seizes the opportunity to lead him onward and upward to higher ground—to make him better acquainted with Christian mercy, fairest of all the graces. "Not," is his reply, "seven times, but seventy times seven"—seventy multiplied by seven. A big number: and yet we would fall far short of the lofty mark if we suppose, that forgiveness is to be confined to the limit of four hundred and ninety insults, wrongs, or robberies. Here, as elsewhere, a definite is employed to express an indefinite number: so that by this expression Jesus taught Peter, and teaches us, that mercy, like the regions of space, has no limit; and that as these stretch away before the traveler who looks out from the farthest star, so the loftiest intellect and largest heart can descry no bounds to mercy. Like our Father in heaven, we are to forgive without stint—forgiving as we expect to be forgiven. And for the purpose of illustrating and of enforcing this truth, our Lord tells the parable of the Unmerciful Servant.

THE MASTER'S TREATMENT OF HIS SERVANT.

He was reckoned with.—As the story runs, the King enters on an inquiry into the way his servants have discharged their trust—an incident, since the King here represents God, which reminds us that He with whom we have to do, will ere long reckon with every man—saying, "Give an account of thy stewardship: thou shalt be no longer steward." God will reckon with us: first, when Death, grim officer of justice, comes to seize man by the throat, and, as he drags him away into the presence of the Judge, seems to say, Pay that thou owest;—and, secondly, when the Archangel, sounding his loud trumpet at the gates of

Death, shall call us from our graves to see the throne set, the books opened, the world wrapped in flames, and God descending in majesty to judgment. But it is neither the hour of death nor the day of judgment which is meant here. Alas! for us, if we are not reckoned with till then. It is too late then—too late to ask for patience; too late to hope for pardon; too late for repentance and return. The door is shut.

> "In the cold grave to which we haste
> There are no acts of pardon past,
> But fixed the doom of all remains,
> And everlasting silence reigns."

It is to the reckoning which God holds with men in time, through His Word, and by the agencies of His Spirit and their consciences, that this parable refers. The King reckons with us, "his servants," when he brings us to a sense of our guilt; sets our sins in dread array before us; impresses us with feelings of contrition, and alarms us with fears of judgment; and by rebukes, corrections, and convictions, pleads with us to flee to Jesus. The bar here is one at which, some time or other, we all have stood; and where, without regard to rank or office, kings and priests, and purest women, as well as the lowest criminals, have been tried. This court holds its sittings within our bosoms —the presiding judge, God's vicegerent, is conscience —the law is the statutes of Heaven—and each man, turning king's evidence, bears witness against himself. And though in a sense man himself here constitutes the whole court,—being at once prosecutor, witness, judge, and jury, and the trial is conducted under circumstances not favorable to an impartial decision,—yet in every case the verdict is, and must be, guilty. We cannot shut our eyes to the fact, that we have all sinned times and ways without number. Whose conscience does not condemn him as a debtor to the law of God? Who boasts, my hands are clean, my heart is pure? The one redeeming feature in that Sanhedrim of sanctimonious hypocrites where Jesus stands facing the guilty woman, is that, when he says "Let him who is without sin cast the first stone at her," a sense of guilt paralyses every arm—they retreat, and she goes scatheless. To say that we have not sinned, is, in fact, to sin in saying it; for we make God a liar, and our mouth proves us perverse. We have all sinned, and come short of the glory of God.

He owed an immense debt.—This is expressed by the very number here—ten thousand, or a myriad, being the highest in the Greek notation. Nor does the debt look less when narrowly examined—being such indeed as could have only been contracted by one who, representing his sovereign in some wealthy province of an Eastern empire, had squandered in boundless extravagance revenues that should have swelled the public treasury. In Roman talents this debt amounts to five millions of our money; and if we reckon by the Jewish talent, and calculate the amount in gold, and not in silver, it rises to a sum equal almost to the whole revenue of the British empire—the servant stands indebted to his master more than seventy millions sterling.

A most enormous sum! but on that account the better fitted to set before a money seeking, making, loving world, in a way suited to its understanding, our enormous guilt in the sight of God. Such is the sum of our transgressions; and representing our debt to the divine law, these figures leave us no hope of being able to pay it—laying on each man a load of guilt enough to sink not one, but ten thousand souls into perdition. That we are guilty, and as debtors to a broken law, are sinners to the extent represented here, is a conclusion so humbling to our pride and alarming to our fears, that we may be unwilling to admit it. Yet better people than we, God's noblest saints, have spoken of the number and guilt of their sins in terms as strong. The man of whom, not partial friends, but God himself said, "there is none like him on the earth, a perfect and an upright man," on seeing his own image in the mirror which God held before his face, started back with horror; and seeming viler in his own eyes than he appeared to his friends when they found him covered with ashes, and his body one loathsome sore, Job exclaimed, "I abhor myself, and repent in dust and ashes." To the same effect is Ezra's confession when, rending his mantle, that man of the highest piety and patriotism threw himself on the ground to cry, "O my God, I am ashamed, and blush to lift up my face to thee, my God, for our iniquities are increased over our head, and our trespass is gone up unto the heavens;" and David's harp sounds forth the same mournful notes, when touching its strings with trembling hand, "the man after God's own heart, lifts his weeping eyes to Heaven, saying, "O, Lord, for thine own name's sake, pardon mine iniquity, for it is great!"

He was bound to pay.—Therefore, seeing "he had not to pay, his lord commanded him to be sold and his wife and children, and all that he had, and payment to be made." This first, as selling a man for debt, and secondly, as involving an innocent family in ruin, looks a hard sentence. It is not necessarily approved of here, and I am not called to justify it; yet, I may remark by way of explanation, that in some countries creditors were allowed to recover their claims by the sale of their debtors. Nor need we hold up our hands in horror at this, seeing, not only that it appears right to compel a man who has obtained another's property by fraud or wasted it by extravagance, to work till he has liquidated the debt, but that once on a time, and not so long ago, in this our own country, debtors were occasionally doomed to a fate more severe. The law allowed their creditors to throw them into jail—not fraudulent debtors only, but those also who under the loss of their fortunes had preserved their integrity—and there, amid the scum and offscourings of society, through malice of enemies or lack of friends, whilst wife and children were left to starve, the unhappy debtor was left to rot. No jail-delivery for him, till a messenger from a higher court—Death—came to set the captive free.

Before considering the bearing of this part of the parable, it may be well to advert to the fact, that this law appears, though under certain important modifications, in the Mosaic code; and that, with such perversion of Holy Scripture as the Devil employed in the Temptation of the Wilderness, men—and, sad to say, even ministers of the Gospel—have used it to defend slavery, and gloss over its abominable crimes. Nature occasionally produces strange monsters—creatures that only excite emotions of terror or disgust, and which, by a merciful law of Providence, rarely prolong their life, and never propagate their species. But in the spectacle of free men, and especially of Christian ministers, standing forth before an astonished world to justify slavery as a divine institution—in a people called Christian, holding that God made one race of human beings to be, like dogs and horses, the servants of another, and, while proposing to erect an empire on the foundations of slavery, with unblushing effrontery and unparalleled blasphemy applying to a system which the Christian world rejects, the sacred words spoken of our dying Lord, "the stone which the builders refused is become the headstone of the corner"—in this what age has produced anything so monstrous as our own? Nothing so cruel to man or insulting to his Maker is found in all history; and, done by men with Bibles in their hands, but without a blush on their cheeks, this offers a most remarkable and terrible illustration of the Saviour's words, If the light that is in you be darkness, how great is that darkness? The whole tone of God's blessed word, its spirit of grace and love, its golden rule, "As ye would that others should do unto you, do ye also to them likewise," are as irreconcilable with slavery as with robbery, or adultery, or murder, or any one of all the crimes of which this system has ever proved the cruel patron and the prolific parent. None—not Satan himself—has more wickedly perverted the word of God than those who attempt to make Jewish servitude an excuse and a defence for modern slavery. So far, for example, as the case in hand is concerned, the debtor who was sold to meet the demands of his creditor had a *right*, by the laws of Moses, to kind and brotherly treatment during the whole period of servitude; and whether the debt was paid out or not, freedom came with the seventh year. In the larger number of cases the bondage was thus no longer than an apprenticeship; and in those few cases where it lasted till the return of the year of jubilee, at the first blast of the trumpet the bondsman went free—"Then," said God, "shall he depart from thee, he and his children with him, and shall return unto the family and possession of his fathers." To pretend that such laws lend any countenance to American slavery, is to insult man's understanding and profane God's word.

Proceeding now to apply the parable, let it be observed that the servant takes no objection to the sentence. He does not challenge its justice: he only proposes to suspend its execution. Drowning men catch at straws. So did he, when, distracted with sudden terror, he cast himself at his master's feet to say—as if ten thousand talents, the revenue of a kingdom, had been but ten thousand pence—Lord, have patience with me, and I will pay thee all! Did he know what he was saying? One can hardly believe it. And yet in undertaking such an impossible task, he was the veritable type of many a sinner. Promising to God never more to commit the sin of which their conscience accuses them, henceforth to keep their hands clean and their hearts pure, they, as it were, undertake, without having one penny, to pay ten thousand talents. So they also do who propose to reconcile themselves to God, and wipe out the guilt of their past sins, by living henceforth lives of blameless obedience. Have patience with me, they say, and then I will pay thee all. Now, suppose that they who have always fallen will fall no more, and that henceforth they will succeed in conquering the temptations which have always conquered them, what then? Keeping out of debt does not liquidate obligations already contracted. What merchant to whom I stand indebted would grant me a discharge on my undertaking hereafter to buy with ready money? To vary the illustration, fancy a man found guilty of murder, on being asked to say why sentence of death should not be passed on him, standing up, and, as a good reason why he should not be hanged, gravely promising to commit no more murders, never more to shed human blood. Some might laugh; none would listen to so absurd a plea. Such, however, is the way in which some sinners propose to pay old debts; it never satisfied man, and cannot satisfy God.

Still, incalculably great though the debt be, there is a way of paying all. It is not by works of righteousness that we have done. He who consents to be a debtor to the grace, will cease to be a debtor to the law of God. Going to prison for us, to bondage for us, to death for us, Jesus, by rendering in his life a perfect obedience to the law, and in his sufferings a perfect satisfaction to the justice of his Father, has paid all. The benefits of his suretyship are ours if we believe. Trembling at the bar, overwhelmed by proofs of guilt, condemned, crushed,—guilty one, lift your head, look up, behold

> "Where high the heavenly temple stands,
> The house of God not made with hands.
> A great High Priest our nature wears;
> The Guardian of mankind appears;
> He who for men their surety stood,
> And poured on earth his precious blood,
> Pursues in heaven his mighty plan,
> The Saviour and the Friend of man."

He was forgiven.—In those old historic straits which join the Mediterranean to the broad Atlantic, there is an upper current from the ocean flowing into the sea, and an under and salter current from the sea which flows out to the ocean; and in like manner the human bosom may, at one and the same time, be moved by the counter-currents of opposing passions—mercy and vengeance; anger and pity; what prompts to punish, and what to pardon. And as in yonder straits all merely floating things, from ships of war to seaweeds, are borne onward of the upper stream, so the fate of one whose crimes excite our anger, but whose misery moves our pity, depends on which of these two passions gets the upper hand—obtains the mastery over us.

Such a case was his whose story forms the groundwork of this parable. His unfaithfulness, and the enormous loss it entailed on a kind and confiding master, called for punishment, and left him no claim to forgiveness. On the other hand, there he was, a miserable wretch—by one sudden turn of Fortune's wheel thrown from its top into the dust, where, as with every bone broken, he lies writhing, crushed by the tremendous fall; none so poor now to do him reverence; by one step he has descended from a proud position to stand, with a wife and children whom his crimes have hurried into ruin, in the auction mart—nothing before him and them but the miseries of lifelong slavery. His heart is wrung with grief; he stands appalled at the prospect; from his fate, pale with terror, and a picture of despair, he shrinks back to throw himself at his master's feet, and implore his pity. "Have patience with me," he cries, "and I will pay thee all." Looking down on this form of abject misery, his master is moved with compassion—"Mercy rejoiceth against judgment." He who asked but patience receives pardon. He who sought but time to toil and save to pay his debts, has them all forgiven. Seeking more than he deserved, he obtains more than he desired. His least fears are disappointed, and his greatest hopes surpassed. Without doing a turn to pay a penny of the sum, the debt of ten thousand talents is at once and entirely cancelled.

Behold a picture of the munificent mercy which God is ready to extend to us—even to the chief of sinners!

Intoxicated with "the cup of devils," many are insensible to their misery; having even "no bonds in their death," they are like that degraded wretch, who stupefied with drink, lies prostrate in the gutter, and, while his family blush with shame and strangers look on with pity, feels neither cold, nor hunger, nor disgrace. But what costs many a gay and thoughtless one no care, moved God to compassion, and brought his Son to the rescue. To save us from sin, and from that hell where they seek for death but cannot find it, and only find after unnumbered ages that their torments are beginning, Jesus interposed, saying, I will save them—suspend the sentence—I come to do thy will, O my God,—deliver from going down to the pit, I have found a ransom—have patience with them, and I will pay thee all!

He paid it. Making atonement for sin, "he was wounded for our transgressions; he was bruised for our iniquities; the chastisement of our peace was upon him; and with his stripes we are healed." The debt was paid on Calvary to the uttermost farthing; and now God only awakens our convictions and alarms our consciences, reckoning with us, that he may bring sinners to acknowledge their guilt, and so prepare them to receive his mercy. Sins are not pardoned till they are acknowledged. If Justice wears a stern aspect; if we think it hard that she will not pass by the smallest sin, that she holds him who offends in one point to be guilty of all, that, like a rough and stern officer, she takes us by the throat, saying, Pay what thou owest, there is Divine love here—" a bright light in the clouds." In dealing with us thus God seeks to bring us to a sense of our sins, that we may flee to the Saviour; breaks down that he may bind up; wounds that he may heal; kills that he may make alive. The upbraidings of conscience, an awful sense of guilt, David's horror when he cried, "The terrors of death compassed me about, and the pains of hell gat hold upon me," are the harbingers of forgiveness. It is as in nature, where lightnings flashing through the horrid gloom and thunders which rend the skies, are preludes of the rain that descends in copious showers on the parched and thirsty ground. Or it is as on that night of old, when a frail and lonely bark, watched by the Saviour's eye, was battling for life in a head wind on the sea of Galilee—Jesus comes in the tempest that agitates the soul. Wrapt in the dark mantle of the night, he advances over the stormy billows; and, ere long filling the troubled heart with a holy calm, his voice is heard, saying, "It is I, be not afraid."

THE SERVANT'S TREATMENT OF HIS FELLOW-SERVANT.

Of the four men lately hanged at Kirkdale, two had seen a man executed for murder but a few weeks before they committed the very same crime. Without sufficiently considering that ardent spirits,—maddened by which both imbrued their hands in blood,—while they weaken the reason, strengthen the passions, and, acting on these as on fire, make them burn with a fiercer heat, people are shocked at such an instance of human depravity. Such a case certainly and awfully illustrates God's question: "Why should ye be stricken any more? ye will revolt more and more"—for, unless checked by the restraints of grace or of providence, correction but exasperates our corruptions, and, producing no other effect on them than fire on clay, hardens rather than softens the heart. The crime of these felons who, swung from the gallows, turn slowly round and round in the wind—a ghastly spectacle, was shocking; yet this servant presents a specimen of humanity in some respects still more detestable. Kindness seems only to have made him more cruel, and generous treatment more selfish; nor do the love and mercy of his lord appear to have produced any other effect on him than the heat of the tropics on poisonous plants and venomous reptiles,—imparting to juices and fangs a deadlier virus. In proof of this, look at his treatment of his fellow-servant!

It is extremely harsh.—If we have civil rights we should use them civilly—refuse even a beggar with courtesy—be kind to all—bear ourselves to the meanest without forgetting that he is a brother, a fellow-creature, one who though less favored by fortune, may carry on his shoulders a better head, and within his bosom a kinder heart, than ours. But this ingrate could not have treated the poor man worse had he been, not his fellow-servant, but his slave; not a debtor, but a robber; not, as probably he was, a man whose infirm health, or numerous family, or unexpected misfortune, had involved him in debt, but one more extravagant in his habits and faithless to his trust than himself. All of a sudden, like a police-officer who lights on some criminal for whom he has been hunting the streets, and haunts and hiding-places of vice, he catches his debtor by the throat, with the peremptory demand, " Pay me that thou owest."

It is most unmerciful.—Though unable to pay the debt, his fellow-servant is too honest to deny it; nor, under feelings of irritation, natural to one treated with such insolence and severity, does he tell this man to keep off hands, and remember, that though he is his creditor, he is not his master,—but a servant as well as he, nor a man so good. Without even attempting to excuse himself, and show how innocently perhaps he fell into debt, the poor man casts himself entirely on his compassion. Though the other, as a servant, was his equal, he stoops to prostrate himself before him as his superior; and, crouching at his feet, makes the same pitiful appeal, that but a few minutes before his creditor himself had made, crying, " Have patience with me, and I will pay thee all!"

Regarding the generous and entire forgiveness of the king which is set forth in the first act of this parable, as illustrating the manner in which God deals with men, in the answer of this servant to his fellow what an illustration have we of David's wisdom when, required to choose between the pestilence in God's hand and the sword in man's, he said: "Let us fall now into the hands of the Lord, for his mercies are great, and not into the hands of man." There is heat locked up in polar ice, and sparks of fire may be struck from the coldest, hardest flint—but there's no pity in this man's bosom. So bad is human nature capable of

becoming; no heart more merciless to man than man's! There was no pity to be expected here—do men gather grapes of thorns? This haughty and heartless upstart could not have incurred such an enormous debt without having passed many years in the indulgence of vice; and all debauchees are selfish—a life of vice resembling those petrifying wells which turn into stone whatever is immersed in them, fairest flowers or finest fruit. The ravages of the worst diseases which vice engenders in the body present a loathsome, but yet a feeble image of the wreck it works on the noblest features of the soul. No wonder, therefore, that this man's heart was not touched by the pitiful appeal—that the only reply to it was, a prison. "He would not," says the story, "but went and cast him into prison, till he should pay the debt."

The circumstances of the unmerciful servant greatly aggravated his guilt.—Good men remember kindnesses, and forget injuries. Doing the reverse, bad men remember injuries, and forget kindnesses—in their hearts, the first are graven on a rock, and the second written in sand. But this merciless servant had not even time to forget the mercy which he himself had received; hardly recovered from his terror, his heart was still beating, as, when the storm is past, the waves continue for a while to roll, thundering on the beach. He had just left the house; he found his fellow-servant at the door; so that when he seized him by the throat, demanding payment and refusing mercy, the whole scene of his own forgiveness must have been fresh on his mind—lying there, though not like the dews that sparkle on every leaf, and bless the flowers they bathe. Himself loved, he should have loved; pitied, he should have pitied; having obtained mercy, he should have shown it. Nor was that all. In ten thousand talents, he had been forgiven much; yet in a hundred pence he refused to forgive little. What was the debt this servant owed him to the enormous debts which he had owed his master? As nothing. And by this the parable teaches us that the debts man owes to us are as nothing to those we owe to God,—that the greatest sins man commits against man are as nothing to those we have committed against God. Those are motes, but these beams; those have their type in the gnat, these in the camel; those are a mole-hill, these a towering mountain, as Ezra says, "grown up unto the heavens;" those are one hundred pence, but these, represented by ten thousand talents, are what it needed the blood of Jesus to pay, and the mercy of God to pardon.

THE RESULT.

When some ruffian man beats a woman, or a grown lad a weeping child, without waiting to inquire into the merits of the quarrel we cry, shame! and even the lowest mob wins our esteem, and lights up its rags with some touch of glory by its promptitude in espousing the side of the weak against the strong; and thus in feelings of indignation at ingratitude, oppression, inhumanity, cruelty, our nature, when fallen into the greatest ruin, still shows some vestiges of the image of God. Under the influence of such a noble anger the other servants, when they saw this poor man seized by the throat and dragged away to prison, went straight to their master and told him of the outrage. They could not right the wrong, he could; nor were they mistaken in believing that he would. He summons the culprit to his presence. His brow grows dark,—the court is awed into silence—as in nature before a burst of thunder, the gloom grows deeper and deeper; and so soon as the culprit appears, his Lord's pent-up indignation launches itself forth on his head, like a thunderbolt, in these words, "O thou wicked servant, I forgave thee all that debt because thou desiredst me; shouldst thou not also have had compassion on thy fellow-servant even as I had pity on thee?" The pardon is instantly cancelled. He is handed over to punishment; and, opening to receive one who parts with hope at its door, the prison closes on him for ever—in other words till, accomplishing an impossibility, he pays the uttermost farthing. And there we leave him, the captive of a prison—the symbol of that place "where their worm shall not die, and neither shall their fire be quenched."

It has been said that no figure walks on all its four feet—in other words, applies in all respects to that which it is employed to illustrate. Christ, for instance, is a Rock; but a rock is dead, while he liveth for evermore—is a lamb; but a lamb is without reason, while he with a true body has a reasonable soul—is a lion; but a lion is savage and blood-thirsty, while he, the express image of God's person, is "very pitiful and of tender mercy." Now this remark applies especially to our Lord's parables, from which, were we to forget that many things in the story form but its surroundings and drapery, we would draw notions the most absurd and doctrines the most unsound. That the king here might illustrate the lesson, With what measure ye mete it shall be measured unto you again, it was necessary to cancel the pardon—crushing this merciless wretch under the load of his original debt. But to infer from that part of the story that such as God has pardoned may notwithstanding be lost, were contrary to his Word and utterly destructive of the believer's peace.

There is enough here as elsewhere to warn us that unless, living a life of faith in Jesus Christ, the branch abide in the vine, it cannot bring forth fruit, and shall be cast into the fire; that the perseverance of the saints is inconsistent with their perseverance in sin— being in fact perseverance, not in course of sin, but in a state of grace. But, type of the sinner who leaves God, this man, as the story runs, "went out." Temptation met him at the door, and he fell, and by his fall teaches us that our safety lies in living near to God, on his bosom—nestled like an infant in the embraces of a mother's arms. Nor, though people may fancy they are pardoned who are not, is the safety of Christ's pardoned ones less secure. By convictions which are mistaken for conversions, and a reformation of the conduct which seems a renewing of the heart, Satan may beguile men, saying, Peace, when there is none to be found; yet our Lord's words shall stand true, "Peace I leave with you, my peace I give unto you; not as the world giveth give I unto you: let not your hearts be troubled, neither be ye afraid." Did he ascend to heaven to prepare mansions for those who might never occupy them? If pardons once past are acts which may be repealed, how could he say of his people, "They shall never perish, neither shall any pluck them out of my hand: my Father which gave them me is greater than all, and no man is able to pluck them out of my Father's hands?" How can angels rejoice when a sinner is converted, if his salvation still hangs in dread suspense, and neither man nor angel can tell but that the bark which, with head turned to the harbor, comes bravely through the roaring sea, may, notwithstanding, strike on the treacherous bar, and be scattered in broken fragments on the beach? Thank God, the covenant is well ordered in all things and sure—" the gifts and calling of God are without repentance."

THE LESSON.

"Forgive us our debts as we forgive our debtors," is a clause in the Lord's prayer, which has in words its best comment in this parable, as it had a very striking one in fact in an event which I happened to witness, —and where the sentence "so likewise shall my heavenly Father do also unto you if ye from your hearts forgive not every one his brother, their trespasses," was, so far as the judgment of the unseen world is ever anticipated in this, fearfully fulfilled. Between a mother and her daughter there had sprung up a serious quarrel. One house could not hold them.

At length filial affection triumphed over pride; and swelling like a dammed up stream till it burst its barriers, nature resumed her course in the daughter's heart. She sought reconciliation. She repaired to her early home. No welcome met her at the door. She humbled herself to her mother, on bended knees imploring her forgiveness. She appealed to the bosom that had nursed her; but might as well have knocked on a coffin—there was no response. Nor, though imploring her by the mercies of God and entreating her to forgive as she desired to be forgiven, could I, called in as a peacemaker, bend that stubborn, iron will. By-and-by, to this lonely home came another visitor. Death, who would not be denied admittance, arrived—summoning her to a bar where they shall have judgment without mercy who have shown no mercy. Called to her dying bed on a night dark, and starless, and stormy, I found the scene within darker than that without. On the floor of the dim and dreary chamber stood a group of pale, trembling, terror-stricken attendants. Death had his victim by the throat; and, with the coldest, cruellest hand of the two, despair had her by the heart. The Bible was there, the offers of mercy there, but no hope—there was no delirium, but the deepest darkness—and, after setting her sins and the Saviour before her, holding up the cross and Christ crucified to her dying eye, I shall never forget, on bending down to ask if she had any hope, the shadow of a hope, the expression of that face. The candle, set in a corner of the bed, shone full on her pallid, sunken, bloodless countenance, and her answer was to throw on me such a look as painters give to the faces of the damned—gnashing her teeth the while. I would not, in any case, claim the prerogative of the judge, nor attempt to raise the curtain which conceals the future, yet no wonder, as I left the scene with shaken nerves, that voices amid the shrieks and howlings of the tempest seemed to sound out these awful words, "There shall be weeping, and wailing, and gnashing of teeth."

Teaching us not to make quarrels, but make them up, to be as ready to forgive others as God is to forgive us, and like him, though the offended, to make overtures of peace to the offender, this parable admits of a wider application. In attempting to heal the wounds and redress the wrongs of humanity, let us learn, from the servants who went and told their king, to tell God of the evils we cannot cure; and let those also who, given up to selfishness, are not touched by the miseries of others, learn that in other things as well as in matters of forgiveness, as they mete, it shall be meted to them. It sounds out this warning, Be pitiless and go unpitied—neglect man's wrongs, and have your own neglected—close your heart to the appeals of misery, and find God's heart closed against you—shut your door in the face of the wretched, and have heaven's shut sternly in your own—live in your selfishness, and die in your sins—be deaf to the wails of earth, and wail in hell—be a curse to man, and be accursed of God! Whether it be bane or blessing which we diffuse around us, let us rest assured that there is a mysterious tide circling in the government of

God that shall, here or hereafter, bring back to us the bread which we have cast upon the waters. It shall return. As men sow, they shall reap. By an infallible decree, they shall have judgment without mercy who have shown no mercy; while those who, Christlike, go about doing good, forgiving such as wrong them, helping such as need, pitying such as suffer, seeking to save others from sin as well as succor them in sorrow, shall, Christ-like also, on leaving the world, go to the Father. Blessed are the merciful, says our Lord, for they shall obtain mercy. Renewed in his image and born again of his Spirit, they are children of God—and so the poet sings:

> "But deep this truth impress'd my mind,
>   Of all his works abroad,
> The heart benevolent and kind,
>   That most resembles God."

XII.

The Parable of the Laborers in the Vineyard.

Matthew xxi. 1—16.

IN this passage of Scripture commentators have found a grand battle-field—all manner of opinions having been entertained, and maintained, about its proper meaning. It forms a part of Christ's answer to Peter's question, "Behold, we have forsaken all, and followed thee; what shall we have therefore?" That is plain: but who the laborers are, what is meant by the hours, what is the true value of the penny, now the story affords either a satisfactory reply to the question that originated it, or a sufficient foundation to the moral that Christ builds on it, are points on which divines have widely differed. The key is yet to be found—if it ever will be found—which, fitting all its wards, will fully unlock this parable. Hitherto it has baffled the efforts of the ablest critics; and in the obscurity under which, to a greater or less extent, it remains, after all that they have done to elucidate its meaning, it stands here recalling the words of David, "I will incline mine ear to a parable, I will open my *dark* saying upon the harp." Rather than attempt to settle controversies which seem insoluble, we shall take a practical view of this parable,—turning our eyes on some great truths which are plainly discernible through what is dusky and ambiguous; and which are calculated, with God's blessing, to reward our attention and, if not to entertain our fancy, to profit our souls. For notwithstanding the doubts, and difficulties, and differences of commentators, this parable resembles a mountain which, though partially concealed by the mists that are wrapped around its bosom and fall in gray folds on its ample limbs, presents in noble forests, and stupendous crags and peaks which, crowned with snow and bathed in sunshine, pierce the skies, many grand views. In opening these up let us first look at the parable as it relates the proceedings of the householder.

His is a story of Eastern life.—He had a vineyard —as indeed have all men of any position or substance in those lands, where vines, planted in the fields, or clothing the naked rocks, or drooping in beautiful festoons from tree to tree, are cultivated, and the grape forms an important article of food, its juice taking the place which milk has in the diet of our farm-laborers, and the fruit of the vine dried in the sun and prepared in various ways besides, forming a means of subsistence the whole year through; facts these from which to learn the true, full meaning of such expressions as "a land of corn and wine," "corn shall make the young men cheerful, and new wine the maids." The time of this parable is that season of the year when, like farms at harvest or at hay-making, the vineyard required more than the work of its regular hands. The householder must hire others; and for that purpose he rises with the dawn, and repairs to the marketplace of the town or village where he resided, and where sun-burned hardy men of bone and muscle on the outlook for employment, were in the habit of assembling. Such stalwart groups may be seen in our own towns; and in the East, where all things are stereotyped, the custom of this householder's time still remains—a recent traveler mentioning that on passing through a town in Palestine, he saw such a gathering in its market-place; and on asking the people why they were standing idle there, got for answer these very words, "because no man hath hired us." Hiring such as he found there at early morn, the householder sent them off to his vineyard, agreeing to pay them a penny for the day's work—a sum which, though it appears small to us, amounting in our money only to sevenpence or eightpence, was the pay of a Roman soldier, and the average wage of a working man. About nine o'clock of the day, here called the third hour, the householder, finding himself still slack of hands, returns to the market-place, and hires others; he does the same at twelve, and the same again at three o'clock,—promising the laborers, since they could have no claim to a full day's wage, to pay them whatsoever was right. By and by the sun sinks low, the day shortens, and the shadows lengthen; another hour, and the chance of an engagement is gone from any who are standing in the market-place Yet once more, late though it be, as with one turned to God when his head is gray, the householder returns; and undertaking to give them also what was right, he hires others, who betake themselves to work, confiding in his justice—perhaps also in his generosity. And now the sun sets; the laborers drop their toil, wipe their brows, and at the summons of the steward come for their hire—the law of Moses, which jealously protected the poor man's rights and leaned rather to the side of the weak than the strong, requiring that the day which saw work done should see it paid. The parable states that the householder directed those to be first paid who were last hired: and so indeed the story required to be constructed—in order to bring forth the bad passions of those who had, to use their own words, borne the heat and burden of the day. Because, had the paying followed the order of the hiring, it is evident that they would have been off to their homes with their wages; nor have had their envy roused by the generosity which made all alike, and, unarrested in its flow by their demerits, bestowed the same wages on such as had wrought one hour as on those who, toiling from morn to night, had wrought all the twelve. These on seeing the last hired receive in a penny the price of a full day's work, fancied that they would receive more. But here, as in other cases, greed cheated herself. They found themselves mistaken: but, instead of swallowing their disappointment to laud the householder, and congratulate their fellows on his generosity to them, they began to murmur against his injustice to themselves. One bolder than

the rest, undertaking to be their mouthpiece, steps out, and, showing the penny in his open palm, remonstrates with the householder, saying, " These last have wrought but one hour, and thou hast made them equal to us, which have borne the heat and burden of the day." They make no appeal to the bountifulness which had lavished its gifts on the others, but, assuming the air of injured men, rest their complaint on grounds of justice. The householder accepts battle on the ground of their own choosing: and how signal their defeat! If they had fulfilled the conditions of the bargain, so had he. They had agreed to accept a penny for the day's work, and he had paid it. Friend, or fellow, he says, I do thee no wrong. If I choose to be generous to others, what is that to thee? It should excite thy admiration, why does it kindle thy envy? Injustice! Is it not lawful for me to do what I will with my own? Begone—away with you and your wages!

Such is the story which our Lord told; and now, to regard it in some of its plain and practical aspects, I remark that we find here

The rejection of the Jews, and admission of the Gentiles.—Fancy, which sometimes roams as wide and wild over the field of parables as over that of prophecy, may think she discovers in the different hours at which the laborers were called, distinctly different periods in the history of the Church—its leading epochs. So in the band which, brushing the dew from the grass, enters the vineyard in the morning, she may see the world's gray fathers, the good men before the flood—in such as were hired at the third hour, the patriarchs who, kindling their torch at Noah's altar, preserved religion alive till the call of Abraham—in their successors, who enter on work when the sun is at his height, the nation that left Egypt to conquer and cast out the inhabitants, and occupy the land, of Canaan—in those summoned at the ninth hour, or three o'clock of our day, the same people, reanimated by a revival under Elijah, or returning under Ezra from captivity to the worship and land of their fathers. Perhaps our Lord, sketching the past with rapid hand, had these events before him: but it is to those of which Time, long pregnant, was on the eve of giving birth, that this parable mainly refers. For many centuries, and all alone, the Jews have been laboring in the Lord's vineyard; while the Gentiles, wholly given up to every species of idolatry, have been standing unhired, and idle,—living without God or hope in the world. The hour of their call being at hand, they were about to be admitted to equal privileges with the Jews: and within the pale of a Church which, made for mankind, was to recognize no external distinctions, knowing men neither as Jew nor Greek, barbarian, Scythian, bond or free; they were to be placed on a level with those who, accounting themselves the meritorious as well as special favorites of Heaven, had looked down with contempt on all other humanity—their boastful cry, "The temple of the Lord, the temple of the Lord, are we." This delightful, glorious prospect was peculiarly obnoxious to the Jews—had no beauty in their jaundiced eyes. Proud and haughty, animated by passions unbecoming fallen man, and most offensive to a gracious and holy God, they rejected both the Scheme and the divine Schemer; and, crucifying the Lord of Glory, were themselves rejected. Filled with pride, scorn, envy, self-righteousness, their eyes open to other's faults but blind to their own, they placed themselves in the same relation to God as these laborers to the householder whose justice they could not justly challenge, but whose generosity to such as, types of the Gentile nations, were called at the eleventh hour, they wickedly and insolently grudged. So, as Christ here and elsewhere teaches, the Jews forfeited the favor of God, and with a "Go thy way," were dismissed from the glorious honors and gracious rewards of his service. Thus, warning us against building our hopes on any outward religious advantages, "the first were last"—as in the adoption of the Gentiles, "the last were first."

A warning against selfishness and self-righteousness.—In the Shorter Catechism of the Westminster Assembly, the answers, as a series of distinct theological propositions, stand independent of the questions to which they are attached; but it is sometimes necessary, in order to fully understand an answer, first to read the question—as in some plants, we find their true substance lodged in the roots from which they spring; and here Peter's question helps to decipher the parable which forms a part of Jesus' answer. A short while before our Lord spake these words, there had occurred one of the saddest and most touching scenes in his history. A young man, liberally endowed with wealth, and, better still, with admirable moral qualities, had, elbowing his way through the crowd, come to Jesus; and, with gaze fixed on heaven and wings outspread for flight, sought his counsel—saying, Good master, what shall I do to inherit eternal life? Go, was the answer, sell all that thou hast and give to the poor, and thou shalt have treasure in heaven; and come, follow me! He was not prepared for this—for such a complete surrender of all which men hold dear. He longed, and looked, and wistfully looked again; but the price was too high. He was unfortunate enough, as others have been, to be very wealthy; and so, though Jesus loved him and followed his departing steps with kindly interest, he returned to the embraces of the world—strange yet true conjunction—"sorrowful, for he had great possessions." What an event for a sermon!—the subject Mammon, and he the text. Seizing the occasion, and taking his eyes from this youth, as with drooping head and slow, reluctant steps, he disappears in the distance, Jesus turns a solemn, sad look on his disciples to say, "Verily I say unto you, that a rich man shall hardly enter the kingdom of heaven. And again I say unto you, It is easier for a camel to go through the eye of a needle, than for a rich man to enter the kingdom of God."

This is a wreck—made, I may say, at the very mouth of the harbor; and not difficult to be accounted for. It can be traced entirely to this, that he acted in the matter from a regard to self, and not to God; and also that he sought eternal life on the score of his own merits, and not on grounds of mercy. Yet hardly has Simon Peter seen the catastrophe, and heard the warning, than, apparently blind to the one and deaf to the other, he comes to his Master with a question, in which we detect distinct traces of a selfish and selfrighteous spirit. He and his companions had not left great possessions to follow Jesus—their "all" being the gains of men who, as fishers, earned a precarious livelihood from the treacherous sea; yet he contrasts himself and them with this youth; and putting in a claim of merit, under cover of devotion to Christ, says, "Behold, we have forsaken all and followed thee;" asking, as if it were not enough to have Him for their reward, "What shall we have therefore?" It needs no chemist's fine tests and delicate analysis to detect base and bad elements in this speech. What shall *we have?* —the question which seems most to interest him is not Christ's honor, but his own profit—what shall we have *therefore* in compensation for our sacrifices; in the shape of wages which we deserve, and you owe to us? "Get thee behind me, Satan," were words with which, like a blow in his face, our Lord once on a time astonished Peter; and it is not less a rebuke of his spirit, and a warning both to him and the others, that Jesus relates a story where those who stand on the value of their works forfeit the master's favor and are dismissed from his service; and where such as work but one hour receive as great a reward as those who toil all day. Thus he teaches that salvation is not of works, but of grace—warning Peter not what he *should*, but what, save for divine grace, he *might* become by indulging the envious, unkind, uncharitable, selfish, and selfrighteous spirit of these laborers; how he would, like the youth of "great possessions," illustrate the saying, "Many are called but few are chosen;" or, like the laborers in the vineyard, the other saying, "The first shall be last, and the last shall be first." Looking, not at its accessories, but main object, this parable could find no better motto than the words of an inspired apostle—so dashing to human pride, but so cheering to the humble and broken-hearted, "Not by works of righteousness that we have done, but according to his mercy he saved us."

Salvation is not of works, but of grace.—Papists and others have drawn the very opposite doctrine from this parable. Misunderstanding or misrepresenting its scope, they have appealed to it as proving that we are saved by works; and that though Christ is, so to speak, the key-stone, our good works form the body and main structure of the arch. In evidence of this, they maintain that heaven is represented here under the form of wages—a reward due to men for their works; and that, of course, those laborers who incurred the householder's displeasure, as well as those who were the objects of his favor and the pensioners of his gracious bounty, represent the saved. If this is so, we have altogether mistaken the nature of heaven and the spirit of its glorified inhabitants. We fancied that it was the abode of happiness, disturbed by no jealousies, embittered by no bad and unhallowed passions—where, though saints, like the stars, might differ in glory, none envied the brighter lustre of others' crowns, but all with one accord, ascribing their salvation to the mercy of the Father and merits of the Son, magnified the grace, none impugning the justice, of God. It is enough to say that an explanation of this parable which, besides contradicting the whole tenor of Scripture, involves such absurdities, introducing envy and jealousy and discontent into heaven, must be wrong. As to the payment of the penny to the murmurers, it is a necessary part of the story. It was a matter of equity on the part of the householder; and had he failed to do that, these grumblers would have had occasion to impeach his justice—not that generosity which is the true point of the parable, the feature of salvation it is set forth to illustrate.

What this parable, where the Church is the vineyard and men are the laborers, intends to illustrate, meets us on the threshold—in the circumstance that the householder, who represents God, seeks the laborers; not they the householder. Early morn does not find them crowding his door, and offering to work in his service: nor even when it becomes known that he has already hired a number, do those who stand idle in the market leave it to repair to the vineyard, soliciting employment. On the contrary, again and again and again, he comes for laborers—in every case the approach and first movement being on his part; never on theirs. Even so, the first steps toward reconciliation between man and God are always taken by Him. He designed redemption in the councils of eternity, so that, in a sense, before man lived he was loved, was redeemed before he sinned, and raised up before he fell. Without any application on our part, of his own free spontaneous will, God sent his Son to redeem, and sends his Spirit to renew. The spark of grace which we have to nurse, He kindled in our bosoms; it was his hand on the helm that turned us round; and whether we were at first, as some are, driven to Christ by terrors, or, as others are, sweetly drawn to Him by the attractions of his love, anyway it was the Lord's doing—Jesus, all praise be to his grace, being at once the Alpha and Omega of salvation, the author as well as finisher of our faith. A great truth this!—it finds fit and glorious expression yonder, where the saints, descending from their heavenly thrones, cast blood-bought crowns at Jesus' feet; and one well put by the simple Christian, who, on being taunted with believing the doctrine of election, replied, "I know that God chose me, because, unless He had first chosen me, I am sure I never would have chosen Him."

Till we enter God's service, all our industry is idleness.—As we have the Church in the vineyard, we have the world in the market-place of this parable: and how striking the picture! There, where some talking with their neighbors tell the news, and some having nothing else to do engage in games, and some are laughing, and some are yawning, and some with their backs to the wall, or stretched out at full length on the ground are sleeping, but none are working, is the world—this busy world, as it is called, where people, believe them, in their daily toil for bread, or keen pursuit of wealth, or pleasure, or fame, have not one hour to spare for the things that belong to salvation and their everlasting peace. Ay, how would many deem us mad, and fancy that religion had turned our brain, were we to walk into the counting-room, the crowded shop, the silent study, the public assembly, to say nothing of the festive hall, the applauding theatre, the gay, whirling ball-room, and address them thus: "Why stand ye here idle all the day?" Mad?—"I am not mad, most noble Festus." There is such a thing as laborious idleness. Busy? So was the shepherd on the Alps, mentioned by Dugald Stewart, who spent fifteen years of life learning to balance a pole on his chin: and the philosopher sagely remarks how much good, had they been directed to a noble object, this diligence and perseverance would have accomplished. Busy? So have I seen the miller's wheel, which went round and round: but idly, grinding no corn. Busy? So, in a way, was the Russian who, facing the winter's cold nor regarding the cost of massive slabs brought at great labor from frozen lake and river, built him an icy palace, within whose glittering, translucent walls, wrapped in furs and shining in jewels, rank and beauty held their revelry, and the bowl and the laugh and the song went round. But with soft breath, and other music, and opening buds, Spring returned; and then before the eyes that had gazed with wonder on the crystal walls of that fairy palace as they gleamed by night with a thousand lights, or flashed with the radiance of gems in the bright sunshine, it dissolved, nor left "a rack behind" —its pleasures, "vanity;" its expense, "vexation of spirit." Busy? So, in a way, are the children who, when the tide is at the ebb, with merry laughter and rosy cheeks and nimble hands build a castle of the moist seasand—the thoughtless urchins, types of lovers of pleasure and of the world, so intent on their work as not to see how the treacherous, silent tide has crept around them, not merely to sap and undermine, and with one rude blow of her billow demolish the work of their hands, but to cut off their retreat to the distant shore, and drown their frantic screams and cries for help in the roar of its remorseless waves. From a death-bed, where all he toiled and sinned and sorrowed for is slipping from his grasp, fading from his view, such will his life seem to the busiest worldling; he spends his strength for nought, and his labor for that which profiteth not. With an eye that pities because it foresees our miserable doom, God calls us from such busy trifling, from a life of laborious idleness, to a service which is as pleasant as it is profitable, as graceful as it is dutiful, saying—Work out your salvation—Work while it is called to-day, seeing that the night cometh when no man can work.

And work now. Why, some may ask, now? Their sun is not yet in his meridian; or, if the shadow has turned, he has still a long bright path to travel ere he sinks in night—eleven hours for play and one hour for work, eleven for enjoyment and one for employment, is their reading of the parable. It is not the right reading. God forbid that I should limit the Holy One of Israel! If one day is with him as a thousand years, so is one moment; and salvation being altogether of mercy and not at all of merit, one last, dim, dying, believing look turned on the cross of Christ, can save a soul on the very brink of—hell passing over into the yawning pit; even as in the camp of Israel "it came to pass that if a serpent had bitten any man, when he beheld the serpent of brass, he lived." True as that is, still the case of the laborers who did not enter the vineyard till the eleventh hour, nor begin to work till the others had begun to think of rest and the coming night, affords no encouragement to procrastination. Admit that these hours, as some think, stand for the different periods of human life—childhood, youth, manhood, and old age, yet let it be observed that the laborers who entered the vineyard at the close of day were never called till then. They had never refused a call—they had no offer till the eleventh hour; and instead of having rejected offers, they accepted the very first they got. None who have read the Bible from childhood, who have heard it preached Sabbath after Sabbath, who have been urged a thousand times by the voices of the dead and of the living to accept of mercy, can reply with these laborers, "No man hath hired us." Their case therefore affords us no encouragement to put off what concerns our salvation, I say not a year or a day, but even a single hour. These rose, responded instantly, to the call. It is not procrastination, but promptitude, therefore, which this parable teaches—promptitude like his who, sinking, drowning in the swollen river, so soon as a rope, spinning out from one who has hurried to the bank, comes within his reach, with sudden and convulsive gripe closes his hand on it; and, holding on like death, is drawn safe to shore. Do thou likewise. Behold, now is the accepted time; behold, now is the day of salvation.

Salvation, though not of works, is for works.— "Show me thy faith by thy works," is the demand of St. James; "Be careful to maintain good works," is the counsel of St. Paul; and the testimony of the whole Bible is, that faith without works is dead. We are not called into the vineyard to sit idle, to fold our hands and go to sleep. They that sleep, sleep in the night; but believers are children of the light and of the day, and have much to do. In amending our habits, in cultivating our hearts, in resisting temptation, in conquering besetting sins, in fighting the good fight, to keep the faith, our banner flying, and, step by step, win the way to heaven, how much have we to do?—so much, that an idle, were as great a contradiction in terms, as a dishonest, a lying, or licentious Christian. In respect even of our own interest and spiritual welfare, may we not use the words of Nehemiah, and say to the world when, with winning smiles or brow of care, it solicits our hearts and time, "I have a great work to do, therefore I cannot come down?" But no man liveth for himself—no Christian, at least: and in a world bleeding from so many wounds, so brimful of sorrow, and suffering, and oppression, and ignorance, and wrong, and crimes, where sinners perish around us as in a great shipwreck, some dashed on the cruel rocks and others drowning in the waves, and all by their dangers crying, Help, we perish!—instead of having nothing to do, might we not wish to have a thousand heads to plan, and a thousand hearts to feel, and a thousand hands to work, the zeal of Paul, the wealth of Solomon, and the years of Methuselah? Let us pity the world; and endeavor, praying and working, so to shine that others, seeing our good works, may be guided to heaven, and glorify our Father there—each such a light, or rather lighthouse, as one of England's bold engineers raised on the reef which owed its dreaded name to the waters that eddied and boiled around it. To save our seamen from a watery grave, their wives from widowhood, their little ones from the miseries and crimes of neglected orphanage, what dangers he faced!—as on that night when, hurrying on deck, he saw white breakers all around, and above their roar and the shrieks of the tempest, heard the helmsman cry, For God's sake, heave hard at that rope, if you mean to save your lives!—and the vessel, with scrimp room to turn, obeyed her helm and rounded off. Example to all who seek a yet higher object—to save men's souls from ignorance, and vice, and hell—what anxieties he felt to bring his enterprise to a happy issue! On the Hoe headland, where Drake first saw Spain's proud Armada, alone in the gray of morning, after a tempestuous night, he might be seen looking out, with telescope at his eye, over a raging sea, for his yet unfinished structure; and heard saying, as a tall white pillar of spray suddenly gleaming on the far horizon revealed his work and removed his fears, Thank God, it stands! Would that Christian men and women were as anxious that God would " establish the work of their hands;" and make each of them, through a loving, active, zealous, pious life, a light shining in a dark place, in a dangerous and perishing world!—such as that lighthouse to the homeward-bound, whose course it guides, and whose hearts leap with joy when, as it rises to the eye of the outlook like a star across the waters, the cry is sung out from the mast-head, and echoed in every cabin, The Eddystone is in sight! Nor do we fear but that they who thus work for God, and Christ, and the good of men, will imitate Smeaton in giving the glory where the glory is due—inscribing on their lives the words which, as the last work of the mason's chisel, he had cut on that monument of his genius and humanity, *LAUS DEO*—praise to God! A fitting motto these for the heavenly crown; and also for a life on earth which, founded on the Rock of Ages, and built up through grace amid many trials, hardships, and storms of temptation, has been blessed of God to guide the heavenward-bound to their desired haven, and, by shining on their way to Jesus, to save those that were ready to perish!